Praise f

"*Your Deepest Ground* is a b
cate process of embodying o

Adyashanti
author of *Falling into Grace*

"This beautiful and deeply insightful work invites us to reconnect with our true ground—a place of inner stability and peace that lies beyond fear. Drawing on decades of experience as both a psychotherapist and spiritual teacher, John Prendergast offers practical wisdom for connecting with a deep, unshakable sense of well-being. This book is a gift—a tender companion for those who wish to live with an open heart and find freedom in the simple, steady presence of being."

Tara Brach
author of *Radical Acceptance* and *Radical Compassion*

"In this pioneering book, John Prendergast brings us a lifetime of exploration, teaching, and insights into how to heal suffering at its root. *Your Deepest Ground* offers a beautifully written and masterful guidebook that provides us with a clear, contemporary, and exquisitely practical path of nondual wisdom and psychology for embodying our innate wholeness in our daily lives. The unique addition is not just the bringing together of the mind and heart but also connecting to our gut and the 'ground beneath our body.' If this intrigues you, read this book and enjoy the true gems that will enrich your life."

Loch Kelly, MDiv, LCSW
author of *Shift into Freedom*

"This book is both a lyrical and a knowing guide into the foundational mystery of who we are, the ground of being beyond any identity—lyrical because of Prendergast's intimate, personal voice, knowing and wise in its crystal clarity. The combination makes it a profound pleasure to read and gives a direct contact with the author's own insight rather than with any particular dogma."

Roger Housden
author of *Dropping the Struggle*

"Most teachers of nondual wisdom in the West these days point directly to awakened awareness but neglect to offer guidance on the lifelong journey of embodying this awareness in everyday life. *Your Deepest Ground* points in the other direction: down from the transcendent through the deeper dimensions of our being and ultimately to the groundless ground of connectedness and stability that makes spiritual awakening possible. As both a seasoned psychotherapist and a spiritual teacher, the author has the expertise and experience to lead you on this essential journey, and his groundbreaking new book is a practical, accessible guidebook for the path."

Stephan Bodian
author of *Wake Up Now* and *Beyond Mindfulness*

"*Your Deepest Ground* is a profound exploration of the connection between spirituality and the physical body. Drawing on decades of experience as a psychotherapist and spiritual teacher, Prendergast emphasizes the importance of grounding the spiritual path in our lived, bodily experience. He invites readers to tune in to the wisdom of the body as a gateway to deeper awareness and awakening. He explains grounding in the body and on the earth, as well as in the groundless ground, the vast empty expanse of pure being. This book is important for anyone on the spiritual path."

Lama Palden
author of *Love on Every Breath*

"This is a clear, beautifully written guide to the ground in its many meanings, as our connection to our lower body and to the earth, as our sense of personal safety, and as the boundless spaciousness that encompasses and illuminates our whole being. At the vanguard of both psychological and spiritual understanding, John offers the mature insight of a life dedicated to realizing and teaching the deepest ground. His writing is infused on every page with his deep compassion as a healer and his integrity and wisdom as a spiritual teacher. Highly recommended!"

Judith Blackstone, PhD
author of *The Fullness of the Ground*

"Once again, John masterfully introduces an integrative view of 'inner work' and poses several fertile self-inquiry questions as forms of practice— questions that can open one to the deeply personal, often hidden holdings of one's fabricated self-ground, as well as inquiries that open to the inconceivable, unfabricated ground of being. Which is to say, openness—groundlessness—as such. For those seeking a deeper release of sticky emotional reaction habits and access to the wonderful freedom and ease of embodied groundlessness, this book presents a well-seasoned, easy-access psycho-spiritual approach I wholeheartedly commend."

Ken Bradford, PhD
author of *Opening Yourself*

"You are holding in your hands a book that can open your heart, unearth the psychological veils that may seem to obscure your deepest knowing, and invite your attention to drop into different dimensions of the ground. Though the deepest ground is a timeless mystery that cannot be known by thought, John invites us, through various meditative inquiries, to open to however this mystery may reveal itself experientially. *Your Deepest Ground* is a beautiful companion to John's earlier books, *In Touch* and *The Deep Heart.*"

Dorothy Hunt
author of *Ending the Search*

"In his new work, *Your Deepest Ground*, John Prendergast invites readers into a multilayered, living experience of what it means to be a full human being. In a contemporary spiritual landscape that can too easily become scattered and surface level, Prendergast opens a portal into depth and the inner chambers of the heart. From the basic ground of safety and somatic sensitivity, and all the way through to the liberating majesty of nondual Unity consciousness, his guidebook serves as a wise mentor and loving companion into the mysteries of the sacred world. Enter its inner courtyard and you will find a jewel awaiting you, the radiance of your own Being."

Matt Licata, PhD
author of *A Healing Space*

"This is not just a book—it's an experiential guide that encourages us to touch our deepest fears and transform them into sources of enduring strength. John's approach weaves together depth psychology, spiritual insight, and a lifetime of personal experience. His reflections on the 'ground' offer a compelling reminder of how deeply we need to connect with our core to live with authenticity and love. This book is a beautiful, insightful companion for anyone seeking to live from a place of profound inner security, resilience, and well-being. I find John's work timely, refreshing, and deeply resonant. *Your Deepest Ground* is a gift for all those who are ready to delve into and awaken to the mystery of their true inner ground and foundation."

Richard Miller, PhD
author of *Yoga Nidra*

"Compassionate and wise. Profound yet clear. From the lofty heights of the transcendental self to the deep ground of our bodily being and the tensions we hold there, John Prendergast brings together a lifetime's exploration into the human psyche in a very approachable, down-to-earth style. Best book on the subject I have ever seen. Definitely a keeper. And essential reading for anyone seeking to awaken to their true nature."

Peter Russell
author of *Letting Go of Nothing* and *From Science to God*

"This beautiful book comes from and gently invites us into the depths of our humanity, from which flow the healing, well-being, and awakening we have always longed for. John Prendergast lives in these depths and is a master guide to them and their riches."

Roger Walsh, MD, PhD
professor of psychiatry, University of California, and cohost of the podcast *Deep Transformation*

"*Your Deepest Ground* takes the reader on a profound journey through all levels of awakening. John Prendergast shows us the way to an ever-deepening connection starting with embodiment, then to the deepest dimensions of human consciousness, and ultimately to discover who we really are beyond all form. It's an ambitious undertaking presented effectively by the perfect guide. Prendergast is a master therapist and respected spiritual teacher who shows us a road to genuine freedom."

James Baraz
cofounder of Spirit Rock Meditation Center and coauthor of *Awakening Joy*

"*Your Deepest Ground* not only embodies the truth that we can bring every aspect of our lived experience into our spiritual practice—it shows you how to do it. This is the right time for this book. The right audience? All those who wish to have lives that are in service to a deep understanding of the heart of who we are. If you are heeding such a call, you will reach for this well of truth as a guide again and again. You will return to John Prendergast's wise and gentle embrace until you recognize the embrace as your own."

Caverly Morgan
author of *A Kids Book About Mindfulness* and *The Heart of Who We Are*

"Once in a while, a book comes along that is destined to change the reader's life. John Prendergast's *Your Deepest Ground* is such a book. In these profusely wise and meticulously crafted pages, you will (re)discover the greater wholeness that you may have been partially overlooking. Prendergast's genius lies in his ability to draw the reader to the *experience of the ground*, and not merely to the concept. His prose is clean, crisp, and economical, because he has the lived experience of that which he guides the reader to live in their own lives. To speak simply about something that seems abstract to the mind is a true achievement. This book is a diamond—don't let it slip through your fingers. Give yourself to it wholly, and you will be forever changed."

Jonathan Gustin
founder of Purpose Guides Institute

Your Deepest Ground

Also by John J. Prendergast

The Deep Heart: Our Portal to Presence

*In Touch: How to Tune In to the Inner Guidance
of Your Body and Trust Yourself*

The Sacred Mirror: Nondual Wisdom and Psychotherapy
(with Peter Fenner and Sheila Krystal, eds.)

*Listening from the Heart of Silence: Nondual Wisdom &
Psychotherapy, Volume 2* (with Kenneth Bradford, ed.)

A Guide
to
Embodied
Spirituality

Your
Deepest
Ground

John J. Prendergast, PhD

Foreword by Rick Hanson, PhD

sounds true
BOULDER, COLORADO

Sounds True
Boulder, CO

Published 2025

Cover design by Rachael Murray
Book design by Scribe Inc.

Cover image © 1993 Charles Cramer

Printed in Canada

BK07034

Library of Congress Cataloging-in-Publication Data

Names: Prendergast, John J., 1950– author. | Hanson, Rick (Psychologist), writer of
    foreword.
Title: Your deepest ground : a guide to embodied spirituality / John J. Prendergast,
    Ph.D. ; foreword by Rick Hanson, Ph.D.
Description: Boulder, CO : Sounds True, [2025] | Includes bibliographical references.
Identifiers: LCCN 2024030541 (print) | LCCN 2024030542 (ebook) |
    ISBN 9781649633026 (trade paperback) | ISBN 9781649633033 (ebook)
Subjects: LCSH: Self. | Self-realization. | Grounding (Philosophy) |
    Spiritual life.
Classification: LCC BF697 .P69488 2025 (print) | LCC BF697
    (ebook) | DDC 158.1—dc23/eng/20240822
LC record available at https://lccn.loc.gov/2024030541
LC ebook record available at https://lccn.loc.gov/2024030542

FSC
www.fsc.org
MIX
Paper | Supporting
responsible forestry
FSC® C016245

To you, the reader:
You are already that which you seek.

Contents

Foreword

Every so often you turn a corner in life and find yourself somewhere that feels both new and somehow also already deeply known.

John Prendergast's book is full of such corners, such turning points, as you find yourself drawn again and again into depths of presence and peace. I've known him for many years, and there is no one else who is both so gentle while being so fearless—even fierce—in his commitment to help others live in the depths that are our true home.

"Why bother?" we might ask. The answer lies in knowing that there is more to reality than meets the eye, more than the daily routines, more than the stresses and worries that cloud the mind. We're challenged by many things these days that make us feel uprooted, alienated, ungrounded. Instead, we long to be openhearted, undefended, and undisturbed by the worldly winds. We want to live this happiness even as we raise a family, pursue a career, and build a better a world. We're not sure how. But we do know that there is more to find around the corner.

Both in our ancient spiritual traditions (which certainly include those of Indigenous people) and in modern psychology, there have been many efforts to explore these depths and find what the Buddha called the liberation of the heart. John sorts these efforts into three levels:

- feeling rooted in the earth and comfortable in your own skin

- connecting with the archetypal forces in the outer bounds of the psyche
- resting in the ultimate ground of all in which "we surrender to unbounded openness . . . and encounter an unshakable sense of well-being regardless of circumstances"

As he explores these levels of transformation, the clarity and quiet brilliance of his writing is a real pleasure. Still, John is first and foremost a therapist and a spiritual teacher. He's absolutely serious about bringing us home to the heart. This is a book of practice, not theory, offered by someone who has practiced deeply himself. He offers brief experiential exercises, revelatory conversations, some of his own bumpy lessons, startling insights into the mind, and simple daily ways to live from the deepest ground.

He is an extraordinarily knowledgeable and sensitive guide, and attuned to the fears and blocks that the ordinary mind throws up even as it also reaches for release. He keeps returning to the body, to the pains and joys it holds, and to the deep ancestral wisdom within each of us. This is a very *feeling* book, rich with imagination. He steers clear of scholarly terminology, but I can say that his practices engage powerful neurological processes, including those that give us a sense of stability and place in a shaky world. It's rare to find an author who can both bring you into direct contact with the ultimate transpersonal ground and also offer so much clinically skillful advice about healing trauma.

John is an ardent backpacker, often venturing out into wilderness on his own and sometimes with others. The spirit of that is present as you hear him in these pages: a friendly voice, warm and encouraging, often amused and always curious, steadfast and forward moving while remaining aware of that which doesn't move inside each of us and never leaves us behind. Questing onward, looking ahead with wonder, and inviting us to go with him around the next corner.

Rick Hanson, PhD

Introduction

We all have a subtle yet profound pull to live more from our hearts—our center of love, compassion, gratitude, freedom, and silent wisdom—and less from our heads, the primary source of our critical judgments and core limiting beliefs. Yet to live a truly heart-centered life, we must feel safe. As a result, to live from the heart in a deep and steady way, we must take the time to discover our deepest ground.

I have been exploring the relationship between the heart and the ground for decades, both as a depth psychotherapist, now retired, and as a spiritual teacher. I once thought I could write a single book about both, but I found that the richness of each subject deserved books of their own. I've devoted chapters to the theme of the ground in my previous books *In Touch* and *The Deep Heart*, but here I've taken the space to fully unpack this critically important subject.

Why is the ground—the felt-sense of spacious stability in and beneath the body—so important? In my experience, it is where most spiritual explorers, both beginners and veterans, get stuck, often unknowingly. The ground is largely terra incognita, an unknown territory. There is enormous resistance to exploring it. Why? As in the fanciful maps made by early ocean explorers, there may be dragons there. What are these apparent dragons that hold us back from fully landing *right here* in the middle of our beautiful, challenging, and poignant lives and opening to what is? Survival fear and confusion. We are deeply wired to survive, and we are deeply confused about where our essential safety lies.

Survival fear—the instinctual fear of physical and psychological annihilation—takes many forms, but mostly it draws on our desire to control what we cannot: ourselves, others, and the world. We fear the loss of this illusory control and live with a chronic inner grip of tension, losing touch with our bodies and overly relying on our thinking. We cling to the familiar and avoid the unknown. We believe untrue and unkind stories about ourselves and the world. We try to connect to and belong with others in ways that are superficial and unfulfilling, projecting both our dark and luminous shadows onto others. Above all, we forget who we are and take ourselves to be separate from the whole of life. As a result, we live inauthentically, out of integrity with the depths of who we really are. This leaves an inner ache and sense of lack.

Further, most religious and spiritual traditions reinforce our resistance to opening to the ground and *experientially* facing our survival fears. Most of these traditions focus on the upper half of the body and accent developing the mind or the heart area. The lower half of the body, with its instinctual tendencies of survival, sex, and power, is largely devalued or ignored. There is, however, a growing recognition in contemplative spiritual circles that the region of the belly must be included if we are to authentically embody our spiritual understanding so that it enhances our relationships, work, and care for the planet, the latter of which is in increasingly dire straits. This brings us to the theme of the hara, which means "belly" in Japanese.

The hara, or gut, ranges from the solar plexus to the base of the spine. When I first contemplated writing this book, I thought it would be about the hara as a whole, which is described in Taoism and Japanese martial arts such as aikido. But I soon realized that it was actually the lowest level of the hara—the base of the spine—that was my real focus. In terms of the body, this is where terror localizes. This is where it feels like the rug gets pulled out from under us. This is where we either connect to or cut off from our sense of the ground.

The ground is our felt-sense of support and stability that lies *beneath the body*, and therefore our deepest ground is underground. There are different levels to this sense of being grounded. On one level—the most obvious one—we feel rooted in and connected to the earth. Our bodies are earth-bodies, and we are able to feel this earthy connection. Another level, less frequented, is archetypal. Here we may be pulled down into an underground realm on a mythic journey or contact ancestral conditioning. Shamanistic rituals, vision quests, extraordinary dreams, and plant medicine can sometimes induce contact with this powerful realm. There is a deeper level yet: the ground of being or the groundless ground. Here we surrender to unbounded openness and discover that, in this space, questions of safety or unsafety completely dissolve. When we open to our deepest ground, we encounter an unshakable sense of well-being regardless of circumstances. And our heart, now deeply grounded, is able to fully flower like a lotus with its roots deeply anchored in the mud. We feel in deep integrity with ourself.

There is also a false ground, the ground of the apparent separate self or "little me." This ground is a contraction, a frozen place, much like a thin layer of ice over a body of water. As a separate self, we can sometimes sense that we are skating on this thin ice. This false ground is a chronic grip of inner tension that defends against opening to our true ground. It is a bundle of false beliefs, reactive feelings, and somatic contractions that we mis-take to be ourself. We unconsciously cling to it because it is familiar, choosing a known suffering over an unknown openness. As a result, we assume that, except for brief respites, feeling anxious, depressed, alienated, and disconnected is all that life offers. We habituate to feeling separate and inwardly contracted. Finding our true ground requires that we see through this false ground. Seeing through what is false allows a spontaneous letting go and unfolding of what is true.

My approach to the ground may be surprising to some since it includes dimensions that are not usually included or combined. It involves a blend of contemporary depth psychotherapy, energetic sensitivity, and nondual understanding based upon direct experience. In my view, at least one of these important dimensions often gets left out of teachings about spiritual development. My psychotherapeutic understanding comes from over four decades of practicing adult individual psychotherapy as well as from supervising and training masters-level counseling students for twenty-three years. My energetic sensitivity first emerged in late boyhood and blossomed once I began a regular meditation practice and started working with clients. My nondual understanding unfolded after many years of meditation and self-inquiry and was catalyzed by years of close study, first with the European sage Jean Klein and then with the American spiritual teacher Adyashanti.

How to Approach This Book

As you read this book, pay attention to your body, especially to the felt-sense in your pelvis and below. Be willing to be surprised. Your subtle sensitivity is also listening as you read! I also invite you to approach this book as an experiential guide. While the concepts here offer a helpful map, you will need to put them into practice to realize their transformative potential. The guided inquiries and meditations assist this. Try them out several times, particularly those that are most resonant, and adapt them as you see fit. Make yourself comfortable. I suggest that you record them with appropriate pauses on your smartphone. Don't just be a curious onlooker; really dive into this exploration. The point is to embody this understanding so you know it in your bones.

All of the anecdotes, conversations, and brief case studies that I share in this book are real. In most cases, I've changed names and masked identities. The exceptions are in chapters 3, 11, and 16 where, with permission, I have used real names. These accounts are broadly representative of both beginners and seasoned explorers as they open to their ground and make genuine in-the-moment discoveries. My hope is that this approach encourages you to find out what is true for you.

The book is divided into three sections, partially following the classic structure of the underworld journey. In part 1, entitled "The Preparation," I offer you a map of the territory, suggestions for an optimal attitude, and some highly useful resources for your journey. In part 2, entitled "The Descent," I invite you to question your false ground, recognize and welcome your deepest fears, let yourself fall open, and discover the groundless ground. I also discuss the role of the collective unconscious pioneered by the founder of analytical psychology Carl Jung. In part 3, entitled "Embodying Spirit," I describe how discovering your deepest ground impacts your ordinary life and radiates out into the greater field.

A Personal Note

I will be in my midseventies when this book is published. It is almost certainly my last. As such, it feels like a final flowering and offering. I pass this understanding on to you with empty, weathered hands formed in a bow of gratitude. Consider it like an open love letter you found lying on the ground.

May you be peaceful, happy, deeply at ease, and filled with gratitude. May you spontaneously and generously share this embodied understanding with those around you. And may you take care of this precious blue jewel of a planet for the generations of beings, human and otherwise, that follow.

Part 1

THE PREPARATION

Map, Attitude, and Inner Resources

Opening to the ground is a lifelong journey. The better equipped we are at the onset, the easier it is to traverse. Having a relatively clear map of the territory helps us deal with the inner mountains, frozen plains, deserts, swamps, and obscure trails as they arise. Having the right attitude—the willingness to be intimate with our experience rather than trying to change it—keeps us from getting stuck in one place.

Further, attuning with spacious awareness or presence allows for an authentic welcoming of our experience. Decoding our sense of inner knowing taps into the wisdom of the body, a highly trustworthy source of subtle guidance. And learning to recognize, skillfully question, and see through our core limiting beliefs allows the upwelling light of awareness to more directly imbue our conditioned body-mind.

As a seasoned backpacker, I know the value of careful preparation before embarking upon a long ramble in the wilderness. This section reviews the most important resources you'll need on your inner journey down and in.

1

Embodying the Ground

Inside of you and inside of everyone, reality is moving to
wake all of itself up to itself. Everything within our human
structure is going to be uncovered in the process.

—Adyashanti, *The End of Your World*

W hat does it mean to embody spirit? Most simply, it means to
recognize and live in accord with our true nature as spacious,
loving awareness. It also means that our deepest knowing is visceral
and vibrant and that our ordinary life is increasingly congruent with
this knowing. For this deep embodiment to take place, we need a
clear mind, an open heart, and a spacious sense of the ground. If the
first great step of the inner spiritual pilgrimage is from the head to

the heart, the next step is from the heart to the ground. This is a natural descent of awareness down and into the body that is profoundly liberating. Opening to the ground is a poorly understood yet critically important part of the spiritual quest. Despite its importance, relatively little has been explicitly taught or written about it, especially for the Western spiritual practitioner. The primary reason for this has been the unconscious fear of annihilation that arises if a deep letting go is allowed.

In my over forty years of inner work with students and clients, the subjective presence or absence of inner ground has been the most important theme I've worked with. I've repeatedly observed how people's inner process of deepening and opening up is sabotaged by their terror of letting go. People really struggle to navigate this murky area (examples to come in subsequent chapters). Mature spiritual explorers become mired here for years. Perhaps you are one of them? With this book I shed some light on this obscure, difficult-to-navigate territory. A bit of clear guidance can go a long way!

The psychological conditioning that obscures our clear access to the ground is both dense and charged. This conditioning is hard to approach experientially because it threatens the mind's illusion of control and often deeply impacts the nervous system. The portal to the ground usually lies within the shadow of fear. As we face our fears, we find our ground.

Many cultures have myths about a difficult underground descent marked by intense challenges and great discoveries, by death and rebirth. In these myths, the underworld is often a hell realm where the hero must confront and overcome demigods or demons, some quite graphically described. In the Greek myth, a heartbroken Orpheus descends into the underworld to retrieve his lover Euridyce, who died from a snakebite on their wedding day. First, though, he has to charm Hades, the god of hell, to gain entrance. In *The Divine Comedy*, written in the early fourteenth century, Dante Alighieri depicts his encounter with an enormous three-headed devil with bat-like wings that lives at the very bottom of a hellish inferno. Interestingly, everything there is frozen in ice since it is farthest from the warmth and light of the sun. While the devil munches on the great betrayer Judas, Dante must crawl down "the shaggy coat of the king demon" in order to leave and enter Purgatorio, the next phase of the spiritual journey. We see a modern version of this story in J. R. R. Tolkien's *Lord of the Rings*, where Gandalf grapples with the terrifying underground demon Balrog as they plunge into a dark abyss. He disappears for a long while, then returns brilliantly transfigured. It's a compelling metaphor: the descent into darkness that often precedes an ascent into light. And it is a theme we will return to repeatedly in this book.

The human psyche has been pointing us toward this seemingly perilous descent as long as we have dreamed and shared stories. At some point we must all crawl down the shaggy coat of our human conditioning in order to discover a more profound reality. Yet we often fear that opening to this underground dimension will bring terror, the loss of control, disconnection, and annihilation. Who wants to go there? In truth, this journey is rarely as difficult as we imagine.

Because of our individual and collective avoidance, our sense of the ground remains largely unconscious and *underground*. We do not realize how deeply ungrounded we actually are. We do not see how driven we are by fear—both physical and psychological—and how shaky our foundations are.

Survival fear is the undertone of our fragile human lives. If we step back and carefully observe, we can see how we organize our lives around trying to be safe. We unconsciously protect our bodies *and* our self-images. The two are intimately interwoven because we are social beings. We need food, shelter, physical safety, touch, *and* a secure connection to others. As much as we prize our individual freedom, at our core we are deeply tribal. This means we strive to be valued and loved by others, and therefore we unconsciously fear rejection, exclusion, disability, and death. Maintaining an acceptable self-image, one that is valued by the community, is a core survival strategy. As a result, we create elaborate defenses, many of them unconscious, to protect ourselves.

The fear of annihilation is the greatest saboteur of the spiritual quest. We want to be loved and feel safe. Generally, the spiritual quest severely challenges both of these goals, at least as they are conventionally understood. In fact, as we deepen in our spiritual understanding, we eventually come to realize that this fear is unfounded. We *are* the love we seek, and our fundamental nature can never be harmed. Yet these are hard-earned experiential insights that require a profound letting go and opening up that only come from honestly facing our experience just as it is and deeply inquiring into who we really are.

The Ground Defined (Lightly)

I define the ground subjectively as a vibrant *felt-sense* of space and stability that encompasses the lower belly and the area beneath the body. We can sense the presence or absence of this ground in the interior of our body. The words *ground* and *space* rarely dance well together, but here they do nicely. When we are deeply grounded, the lower belly feels alive and there is a sense of having landed in oneself. Conversely, when we are ungrounded, we may feel cut off, numb, or subtly shaky at our base, as if the rug could be pulled out from under us at any moment. I'm sure you've experienced this at some point in your life; I certainly have. I suspect this is one reason why earthquakes are so unsettling. They reflect how unstable our conditioned inner ground actually is.

Beyond the physical body, I am also using ground as a metaphor for various levels of reality. In this sense, we can be both relatively and absolutely grounded. The relative ground refers to being conscious of our thoughts, feelings, and sensations—whether gross or subtle. For example, if we are mentally grounded, we are not lost in our thoughts and we are able to think clearly. If we are emotionally grounded, we can experience our reactive feelings without being absorbed in them and also feel love, gratitude, appreciation, grief, empathy, and compassion. If we are physically grounded, we can feel our body regardless of its health or capabilities, love being in nature, and feel at home in the physical world. If we are subtly grounded, we can sense the subtle energies in the interior of our body as well as our subtle interconnectedness with others. We may also connect with archetypal energies of the collective unconscious, as Carl Jung described in his strange, tumultuous, and seminal *The Red Book*. Overall, the more we are in touch with our relative reality, the more relatively grounded we feel.

The absolute ground refers to the groundless ground or ground of being. This is the source of everything that appears, all of our experiences, the domain of pure potentiality, what we may call the deepest "reality." It feels both empty and full. Since this groundless ground is not an object, it is ungraspable by the ordinary mind. We literally cannot wrap our minds around it. It is before all experience and empty of all definitions, stories, and images. It is not a thing; it is no-thing or a non-thing. It is not even an "it." It is nonlocatable, prior to space and time. Yet every "thing" arises from and returns to it, like the waves of an ocean. We can know it by consciously being it. If this sounds completely abstract and puzzling, that's okay. You'll likely get a better sense of it as you read further, especially if you engage with some of the inquiries and meditations provided.

We call the absolute ground many things—the Radiant Void, Godhead, Tao, Buddha Nature, Christ Consciousness, or the Great Mystery, to name a few. It doesn't matter, though, since words and thoughts cannot define it. We know it directly via inner silence and stillness, by being aware that we are aware. Jean Klein, my first foundational teacher, called it our home ground because when we consciously recognize it, we feel profoundly at home. We feel a deep inner stability, ease, and sense of well-being no matter what is happening in our life. When we are in touch with absolute reality, we feel absolutely grounded.

Reality is inherently grounding when we accept it. The more in touch with it and accepting we are, the more grounded we feel. Yet reality is ungrounding if we do not accept and live in accord with it. If we pretend to be someone we are not, we will feel ungrounded. If we are in a relationship with someone or engaged in work that is deeply incongruent, it will be unsettling to face this reality, at least at first.

The truth is disruptive to any individual or collective system that is based upon its denial. As a result, we may first experience a period of disorientation on the spiritual quest before we reorient to a deeper, more authentic life. It depends upon how honest we've been with ourselves. Regardless of our work and relationships, if we take ourself as a separate self, as a solitary fragment disconnected from the whole of life, we will find ourself living in an unstable daydream. Life has a way of waking us up from this illusion, though sometimes quite rudely.

My Journey with the Ground

My journey of opening to the ground has been gradual. While the opening of the mind and heart happened fairly close to each other in my early fifties, the opening of the ground has been much slower. This seems to be the case with most people. It is as if the dirty dishes of my underground conditioning have been soaking in presence for years. Occasionally residues soften and old knots release. For example, it has felt like subtle layers of tension in my solar plexus and the base of my spine have been slowly melting and releasing for years. In my experience, it takes time for the light of awareness to penetrate and transform these denser layers of the body-mind. As this happens, we become more like an attuned musical instrument that can sound in uniquely creative ways or like a stained glass window that allows a primal light to shine through and refract in distinctive colors.

We are all being worked on by a greater intelligence, whether we realize it or not. Occasionally we have glimpses and foretastes of this unfolding process. For example, the theme of this book was foreshadowed nearly fifty years ago while I was on a long meditation retreat in the Swiss Alps. During an especially deep meditation I saw a brilliant, multicolored light bridge spanning the earth and the heavens—a rainbow bridge. While I recognized that it was an important image, at the time I only dimly intuited its meaning. Looking back, I now recognize that it was the seed form of my life's work—to illuminate the importance of the body as we embody our deepest understanding.

Since those early days of long meditation retreats, I've discovered that the body acts as a bridge between the relative and absolute levels of reality, between the earth and the sky, between form and formlessness. As we let go of who we think and feel we are and what our body is, the body opens up and an underlying seamlessness reveals itself. We discover that our body, along with the most ordinary moments and objects of life, are sacred expressions of our innate wholeness.

As I explore the theme of the ground with you in this book, I will describe this sacred ordinariness—this nonseparateness of spirit and matter—as vividly as I can and invite you to discover the truth of it for yourself. This discovery changes the way we individually live and, if enough people participate, how we live collectively. It is a shift from living on the surface of our life to living from the deep ground.

The Challenge of Embodying Our Spiritual Understanding

Many of us have discovered that our true nature is open, wise, and loving, and yet we act otherwise, getting lost in our old stories and emotional reactions. We forget who we are and act out. Have you ever wondered, *Why is this still happening?*

Part of the answer is that we are all deeply conditioned human beings, and some degree of forgetting and reactivity will always happen as long as we are in a body. In my view, despite our idealized images of saints and sages, it is unrealistic to think that we will ever be reaction-free. Recognizing this allows us to relax whatever self-perfection project we may be caught in. However, I do think it is realistic to expect that, as our spiritual understanding deepens, we will react less. That's been my experience. My feathers still get ruffled from time to time but far less frequently or intensely these days.

Our conditioning runs deep—very deep. And it resides on many levels, most of which are unconscious. An iceberg is a good metaphor for this since the bulk of our conditioning is frozen below the surface of the conscious mind. It shows up as subconscious core limiting beliefs, reactive emotions, and somatic contractions, forming an interactive bundle that fuels one another. For example, regardless of conscious understanding, if we subconsciously believe that we are unworthy, we will also feel ashamed and likely experience a clench somewhere in our body, usually in the heart area or gut. Often a limiting belief is the primary trigger for the reactive emotion. Sometimes, however, when difficult conditioning happens early on, such as trauma or a broken or weak relationship with a primary caretaker, a deep imprint is left upon the nervous system and body prior to any conscious thought. These take time—sometimes a long time—and often an attuned relationship to melt and unwind.

Our varied conditioning—whether from our childhood, our familial and cultural ancestors, or our shared experience as human beings—acts as veils that prohibit us from recognizing and embodying our true nature. Along with normal human developmental stages, this conditioning reinforces the illusion of being a separate self, disconnected from the whole of life.

Occasionally, these veils briefly part and we have a glimpse of our natural way of being—whole, intimate with all of life, inwardly free, peaceful, clear, loving, joyful, and grateful for no reason. These openings can happen spontaneously at any time—as children or adults, in nature, during meditation, in the presence of a genuine teacher, under extreme duress, or during a guided medicine journey. Indigenous peoples have sacramentally used psychedelics for millennia to peer behind these veils, and as such, psychedelics have become a common first door into temporary ego transcendence for several generations of Westerners.

These glimpses behind the veils are very useful. They reveal what is most deeply true. Once we know ourself outside of the apparent prison of the separate self, we are less likely to fall under its spell. A spark has been ignited. We may also sense this inner radiance without a dramatic glimpse and simply be drawn by a quiet knowing that there's more to life than what we think and see. One way or another, a search ensues and we begin to find our way home.

We are called to find out who we really are, which requires a careful investigation into who we have mis-taken ourself to be. Almost always, we will need to clearly see and see through a number of multilayered veils. As these veils thin, the light grows stronger. And as the light grows stronger, it is easier to see through the veils. The mind, heart, and body become more open and illumined, and as a result, we increasingly embody the light of awareness.

At some point a gravitational shift in identity may happen when we firmly know we are not bound by any identity. We are aware that we are aware, and we rest in and as this light of awareness. Instead of thinking and feeling *I am this image or story*, we realize an unconditioned sense of being. We can call this self-recognition or a spiritual awakening. When this shift happens, we are clear that awareness is the context and core of every experience. No matter what we experience—any particular thought, feeling, or sensation—we are also present *as* open, unqualified, and undefined awareness. If we have been vacationing with awareness for a while—that is, visiting it from time to time—we realize it is not just a pleasant and expansive state; rather, it is our home ground.

To know ourself so clearly, however, does not mean that this knowing automatically transposes to our ordinary life of relationships and work. It can take a while for the conditioned body-mind to catch up—a lifetime, in fact. There may be a large gap at first. This process of embodiment both precedes and follows self-recognition. A spiritual awakening of this magnitude is a catalyst. Whether pre- or post-awakening, the light of awareness increasingly imbues and transforms the conditioned body-mind.

Sourced increasingly in presence, when we rigorously question all of our disturbing thoughts as they arise and fully welcome our reactive feelings and constricted sensations with curiosity and affection and without an agenda to change or get rid of them, the gap between our deepest knowing and our ordinary human life closes. This book is about this open-ended process of embodiment, particularly as it relates to our densest resistance to opening to the ground.

Initial spiritual glimpses or awakenings are like flying coast to coast, where we are able to get a clear view of the passing landscape from thirty thousand feet. Embodying this understanding, however, is like crossing the land by foot. We get to have an intimate contact with the plains, rivers, mountains, deserts, and oceans—and their many inhabitants. We get to walk our talk close to the ground.

2

Opening the Head, Heart, and Ground

Though silent, it sings.
Though dark, it is luminous.
Though still, it dances.

Every experience—any thought, feeling, or sensation—can be a portal to discovering our true nature. If you explore your experience deep enough, you will discover a vibrant, wakeful silence in its core. In my experience, and that of other contemplative traditions and teachers, there are three major doors to access our true nature: the head, the heart area, and the lower belly/base of the spine. These doors roughly correspond to our capacity to think, feel, and sense. Although we are accessing the same awareness through each of these doors, they all accent different essential qualities of being.

The Head

When we access open awareness through the mind, we often experience great clarity, a profound inner freedom from all definitions, and the sense of a vast, sky-like space around and above our head. We're able to recognize that the long-standing and compelling personal narrative that *I am so-and-so, who was born to these parents in this place, who does this work, and is related to these people* is a facade. The facts are correct, but the interpretation is not. We realize that our biography, while relatively true, does not fundamentally describe or define who we really are. Though we remember our personal narrative, we are not bound to it. This awakening from the mind is often facilitated by careful self-inquiry and silent, open meditation. Sometimes this recognition arises spontaneously but, more commonly, it arises with the help of an experienced guide.

We know our self as no one—free of all labels, identities, and beliefs, even as we continue our ordinary and uniquely expressed life. Knowing that we are no one, we are free to be as we are. When the ego has been dethroned, the throne remains empty and open. We don't need to change our work or relationships unless they are obviously incongruent with our unveiled knowing. The ordinary mind functions more economically and creatively without the burden of believing that it runs the big show. It becomes comfortable with not knowing what it can't know (such as what's going to happen next) and settles down to become an excellent administrative assistant to our deepest knowing. When spiritual teachers or teachings describe our true nature in this way, they are speaking about the awakened mind. It is a powerful and important opening, but it is also incomplete. We can sense this because awareness still tends to localize above the head, albeit spaciously, and we feel subtly "top-heavy." Further, most of our emotions and instinctual impulses have not been affected by the opening of the mind and, as a result, personal relationships continue to be unsettled and challenging.

The Heart

When we access open awareness through the heart, we experience an all-embracing, unconditional love of what is. I describe this intimate, multidimensional exploration and discovery in my prior book *The Deep Heart*. Many of the principles and practices that I introduced there, such as the evocation of presence in order to be intimate with experience and the importance of questioning our core limiting beliefs, apply equally well to our exploration of the ground. Not surprisingly, the willingness to be vulnerable and honest with ourself is also relevant and helpful. As we identify and see through veils of illusion that cover the depths of the heart, deeper layers of sensitivity, feeling, and understanding naturally unfold. And as we come into more intimate and accepting contact with our conditioned human heart, we eventually come to realize that we are essentially whole, regardless of our human flaws and limitations, and we feel this inherent wholeness in others. We also deeply know and feel our non-separateness from everyone and everything. Any remaining sense of duality between an infinite knower and a finite world dissolves. There is no longer a knower and a known; there is only knowing.

As the heart area awakens, we also increasingly feel a causeless love, joy, and gratitude. There is an upwelling and outpouring of kindness and compassion. This opening is often associated with the archetype of the Great Mother, the one who holds the suffering of humanity in her infinite heart. When teachers or teachings describe awareness in these terms, they are speaking about the awakened heart. While many spiritual teachings stop here, there is a further step for aware-ness to completely unfold: down and into the ground. Until awareness descends all of the way down and through the body, it is difficult to sustain a deep openheartedness. Unconscious fear continues to under-mine a full embrace of life as it is.

The Ground

When we access awareness through the lower belly and the base of the spine, we are opening into a domain that is darkly mysterious to the mind; we are opening to the unknown. I'll explain how to navigate this descent in part 2. This domain is prior to any thought, even the thought *I am*. Here we can sense a profound, unchanging stability and a feeling that all is well, no matter what. Descriptions are often paradoxical and poetic:

> Though silent, it sings.
> Though dark, it is luminous.
> Though still, it dances.

We can feel an essential life force welling up from the infinite depths of this ground, a life current that animates all beings. There is a clear sense of verticality, of inner alignment. When teachers or teachings describe awareness in these terms, they are referring to the awakened ground.

The opening of these three doors—head, heart, and ground—is nonlinear. They rarely unfold in strict sequential order. That said, embodiment most commonly unfolds more or less downward, as if awareness is descending into and through the body. Having initially transcended our personal narrative in the mind, there is a natural movement of awareness down and in. We wake down.

An opening in one of these three main centers will catalyze an opening in another center in subtle and unpredictable ways. For instance, an opening of the head allows attention to more easily drop into the heart, and the opening of the heart may allow us to see through an old belief that we are unlovable. As our sense of ground deepens and steadies, it will feel safer to open our heart and examine other core identities. As we see through our false ground and instinctual dimensions of our conditioned identity, the mind, heart, and authentic ground further open. We feel ourself become more open-minded, openhearted, and open-bodied.

In my experience, this unfolding process is different for each of us and depends upon our unique conditioning and personality. Because of this, it is good to keep an open mind about how it unfolds and continue to deeply listen in the moment to sense and be with what is opening or wanting to open.

Coming into Integrity

Why is becoming aware of our ground so important? It is a matter of integrity. If we are honest with ourself, we are more willing to face and lean into where our life is not in alignment with our deepest knowing, not in order to have a shinier image of our self but to embody our spiritual understanding. There is a primal desire in all of us to be more authentic. There is also a desire to be a clear and loving servant of the whole. The two are linked, for the more truly authentic we are, the more we are naturally in service to a life beyond our egocentricity. This will look different for each of us. Whether we are tending our local garden of relationships or sharing on a communal level, we will be moved by a grounded love and wisdom when we stand in our integrity. The effect will always be benevolent.

Meditation
Sensing the Ground

Find a quiet place where you won't be disturbed. If possible, sit comfortably upright with your feet on the floor or your legs comfortably folded. Otherwise, find a comfortable relaxed position. Close your eyes or leave them slightly open and take several deep, slow breaths.

Begin by reminding yourself that there is nothing to fix or change in your current experience, and there is nothing to achieve for the next few minutes. It is enough to simply be as you are.

Allow your attention to settle down and into the core of your body as you breathe. This will happen naturally as your mind realizes it has no work to do.

Feel the weight of your body being held by whatever you are sitting upon. Relax into the sense of being physically held.

Bring your attention to your breath and imagine that you can inhale and exhale directly from the ground beneath your body. Allow your exhalation to completely empty out into the underground space. Wait for the inhalation from the depths of the ground to come on its own.

As you exhale, feel how open this underground space actually is.

Continue to sit for at least ten minutes, sensing into this underground space as you breathe. If your attention wanders, simply bring it back to your grounding breath.

When you're finished with your practice, slowly open your eyes and rest for a minute or two before getting up. Take note of how it feels to be in touch with the ground before you reenter your activity.

3

Self-Honesty and Vulnerability

A condition of complete simplicity,
(Costing not less than everything)

—T. S. Eliot, *Four Quartets*

Opening to our deepest ground requires that our attention drop all the way down through the body. It is a process of unveiling, unlearning, and emptying out—a deep letting go. How does such a process strike you? Most of us have mixed feelings about it. The strategic mind wants to know what we will get out of it. What is the benefit of risking "not less than everything," as the poet T. S. Eliot writes? Yet this invitation is not from or for the ordinary mind that loves to bargain and strategize. Rather, it is the call from the heart, the very core of our being. It is the intuition of greater freedom, aliveness, authenticity, and love. If we are honest, we will acknowledge that we both want and fear such openness.

It's important to be honest about our fears. In this approach, we face them and embrace our resistance with compassionate self-honesty and vulnerability. This attitude is more important than any spiritual principle or practice because if we are not genuinely willing to be honest and vulnerable, especially with ourself, our discovery process will stall. Honesty compels us to face our experience just as it is. Vulnerability allows us to open to and explore it.

This exploration into our deep ground is a bit like entering a dark cave. In many shamanic traditions, the journey to the lower world begins by finding a hole in the ground, a hollow tree, a sinkhole, or a waterfall. In dreams we may find ourself perched above a steep cliff, peering into a dark abyss. Whatever the imagery, this part of the journey is clearly an underground descent. Yet unlike modern cave explorers, we do not enter equipped with elaborate ropes, carabiners, and headlamps. Instead, we are increasingly stripped down as we feel our way in the dark. At times it can be useful and even essential to have a caving "buddy" nearby—a steady, experienced guide to reassure us and help decode the unfamiliar contours of our experience. In any case, some unseen force draws us down and something in us consents to being taken, even if we are fearful.

This is a path of willingness rather than willfulness. Sometimes this willingness comes after our willfulness has failed. Defeat often precedes surrender. We exhaust the old pathways of seeking pleasure and avoiding pain. Sometimes we need to hit a dead end. Other times we are able to hear and follow the quiet voice of inner knowing that whispers that our life, even a well-adjusted one, is not the whole truth of who we really are. Something in us knows there is more; we sense a hidden depth to our being.

This inner invitation to deepen is not the familiar self-improvement project of the ego. It is not about trying to become a better person, an improved separate self. It is not about being recognized and valued by others as a more competent, charming, knowledgeable, impressive, powerful, or virtuous somebody. It is not about trying to induce states of consciousness, acquire powers, or be special. Instead, it is a call to recognize our true nature and live in accordance with it; to be simple, true, and *fully here*, just as we are.

This is not a path of heroic effort, of somebody trying hard to get somewhere. Rather, it is a path of careful listening and heartfelt inquiry. After all, who is it that is meditating and trying to purify themselves? Who believes that decades of spiritual practice will eventually bear the fruit of inner freedom? Who believes there is somewhere to go and something to get? Who is the one who is believing, searching, praying? *Who or what are you really?* This is the essential question.

The "really" in this question is important because we have all kinds of ideas and feelings about who we are—a rich assortment of identities, some of which are relatively accurate. Yet none of them are essentially true. This is not because we are avoiding or distorting facts about our biography. Rather, it is because no narrative or story, no matter how factually accurate, can define the totality of who we are. The ordinary mind, largely consumed by thought and language, cannot grasp what we really are because who we are is prior to thought.

"Some Hidden Part of Me Is Always Scanning"

A session with Janice, a gifted bodyworker with whom I'd worked closely for several years, illustrates what's possible when we consider who or what we are, really. Even though she had opened deeply to her true nature on multiple occasions and recently felt a clear calling to start a small group to share this understanding, she had not acted on it.

Janice: Maybe I lack commitment.

This did not feel true to me, and I told her so.

Janice: What might it be, then?
John: An excellent question. I invite you to quietly sit with it.

Janice closed her eyes. She took a few slow, deep breaths and allowed her attention to drop down and in for a minute.

Janice: It's fear.
John: Yes, that's my sense, too.
Janice: Fear of what? [*Pause*] The word *annihilation* comes. I won't survive. I can feel a clutch in my belly.

She contracted her hand into a fist at her abdomen to show me what it felt like.

Janice: I have lived this way for most of my life. It's my primary defense. Some hidden part of me is always scanning to see if it is safe to be just as I am. I've never seen this so clearly. Wow!
John: Take a minute and let yourself really see, sense, and feel this core grip.

Janice sat quietly for a while with this multidimensional insight, taking in her long-held, subconscious story with its subtle terror and powerful somatic grip.

John: Ask yourself if it is true *now* that you will be annihilated.

After a brief pause, I watched her face relax and a beautiful smile emerge.

Janice: No, it is definitely *not* true that I will be annihilated if I share my true self now. It feels like my perineum is opening, and I am being filled with light.

She was lighting up from the inside, bottom up.

John: One more question, Janice. Is it true that your true self can ever be annihilated?
Janice: No. It cannot.

She responded with certitude.

This simple yet precisely focused inquiry illustrates the underlying attitude of self-honesty and vulnerability that are the keys to any deep inner investigation. Janice knew that something was holding back a natural flow, and she was willing to intimately explore and experience it. Over the prior months and years, she had gradually recognized her essential being and there was now a natural movement to share this precious discovery with others. She had found a jewel in her core and knew it also lived in everyone. Yet for the part of her that hid quietly in the background—a protective inner guardian that had gradually formed in her childhood and adolescence—sharing this jewel meant risking her life.

This may sound overly dramatic, but it is not. I've encountered this primal fear in many people I've worked with, and I've felt it myself. If we are honest and vulnerable with ourself, we can feel we could die if we let ourself be fully seen by others. We often tend to confuse our sense of self with our body, so if our self-image feels threatened, it can feel as if our physical life is at stake as well. The subjective sense of self is fragile when we are young; we are easily confused and frightened. For several years as a young boy, when I visited my grandparents' old two-story house in an orange grove in Southern California, I'd lay awake for hours afraid of the monsters hiding in the dark corners of my closet. Although the family atmosphere was genuinely benign, my mind found danger in those nighttime spaces and shadows.

In Janice's case, she was very willing to see her primal defense and feel her fear. She needed to clearly experience both the insight and visceral impact on her body. She wasn't trying to fix, change, or get rid of her fear, as uncomfortable as it was. Rather, she was willing to accept and be intimate with it. This was key. Once she intimately experienced her fear, she was ready to question it by asking, *Is it true now?* This question is not just for the rational mind. Certainly she could use her adult mind to find a no. This rational level of response has its value but also its limitation. Subconscious beliefs rarely yield to this level of insight. Instead, her question evoked a knowing that came from her silent depths. It is a knowing that responds intuitively and directly through our whole-body felt-sense, sometimes with words, imagery, feelings, or subtle sensations, and sometimes wordlessly. In Janice's case, there was a clear and immediate no that was accompanied by a spontaneous opening and upwelling of energy at the base of her spine.

She was attuning with the truth. We can be sure of this because her body responded with openness. There was an influx of information and energy that began to quickly transform her closed system. She felt as if she was being filled with light. Her conditioned body-mind was attuning with the light of awareness. It was palpable; we could both feel the shift. The dark basement of her psyche, the bastion of terror, was becoming illumined. It was as if a large window had suddenly opened and sunshine and fresh air had flowed in. She felt a huge relief to be unburdened from her ancient terror and free to be her natural self.

Did this process require effort? Perhaps a little. Janice needed to focus attention into the interior of her body, pose a question, and listen. For some, this may take a little effort and practice. Yet effort was not the key ingredient. Instead, it was her self-honesty and vulnerability that fueled her investigation and bore fruit.

Our earnest dedication to the relative truth of our actual lived experience in the moment—what we feel, sense, and believe—as well as the absolute truth that is prior to any thought is the most important factor in our investigation. Most of us have mixed motives when we engage in this search. I certainly did. We may want the truth, but we may also just want to feel better, which is a common and totally understandable goal. We are ambivalent creatures! If this is true for you, as it is for most people, I invite you to be honest about it. Once we are honest, we can then be curious and begin to deepen in our self-intimacy.

Inquiry
"Do I Really Want to Know What's True?"

Find a quiet place where you won't be disturbed for several minutes. Make yourself comfortable, preferably upright if possible. Take several slow, deep breaths, and let your attention settle down and into your body.

Feel the weight of your body held by whatever you are sitting on and relax into the sense of being held.

Allow yourself to relax into a sense of open space behind your back and take a minute to feel into this openness. Then bring your attention to your heart area in the middle of your chest.

Mentally ask yourself, *Do I really want to know what's true?* Let the question go, and then innocently wait. Avoid going to your thinking mind for an answer.

Simply be open to a spontaneous and natural response. It may come in the form of a subtle sensation, feeling, image, word, or a wordless direct knowing. Whatever it is, let it in.

If there is a predominant sense of open, spacious awareness, simply rest in and as this awareness.

If a clear sense of resistance arises, welcome it without any agenda to fix or change it. Be curious and affectionate. Then notice what happens. Take as much time as you'd like with this insight and experience. When you are ready, get up and go about your day. Continue to be curious and affectionate with your resistance. As you do, it will spontaneously begin to reveal more dimensions.

4

Discovering Presence

In the emptiness of striving and the desire
to achieve, presence is found.

—Jean Klein, *Who Am I? The Sacred Quest*

Our ordinary mind often finds it challenging to welcome resistance. Instead, it is constantly bargaining, either openly or secretly, to get rid of, fix, or change an unpleasant feeling, sensation, or thought. That's its job. Of course we can train our minds to be kinder and more accepting, and there's benefit in doing so. But the conditioned mind will never be able to achieve this. That's above its pay grade. Despite our best efforts, it will always judge and compare. We cannot teach a cat to fetch a stick. When we try to change our experience from the level of the mind, it always falls short. Resistance endures.

For example, if we are working with fear from a purely mental level, it will never fully release. Trying to welcome fear without an agenda to change it is much like welcoming a guest into our home who we secretly hope will leave as soon as possible. Most guests will sense this and refuse to enter. This is not surprising because our "guests"—in this case, challenging emotions like fear, shame, guilt, rage, or worthlessness—are waiting to be received with love and understanding, much like little children. As much as we may be inspired by a poem like the thirteenth-century Persian poet Jalal al-Din Rumi's "The Guest House," we will fail at truly welcoming our guests if they are unwanted, even if we know that "each has been sent as a guide from beyond."[1]

The good news is there is something within us (that is not a thing) that is able to unconditionally welcome and accept our experience just as it is: presence. By presence I mean the sense of being or existing. If we are lost in our busy mind or caught in our reactive feelings, this sense of being will feel vague or absent, yet it is always there quietly in the background whether we consciously recognize it or not.

A quick way to check for this sense of presence is to ask yourself: *Do I know that I exist? If so, how?* Then be quiet and don't think about it. What comes to you? Whatever we may doubt about ourselves, we do not doubt that we exist, that we are. We can't exactly put our finger on why or how, but we know it's true: *Yes, I exist. I am.* This is as true in a dream as it is in the waking state. The more we are in touch with this sense of existing, this sense of being, the greater is our sense of presence. When we are thoroughly convinced that we are not defined or confined by any thought, feeling, or sensation, presence is vibrantly in the foreground of our experience. We can call this a multitude of things, such as a spiritual awakening or an essential recognition; regardless, we know awareness is our true nature. Whether faint or strong, presence is the palpable, sweet, impersonal perfume of this self-awareness.

I say "impersonal" because presence does not refer to or belong to anyone. This may seem strange. How can that which is most intimate and true about ourself not be personal? Because we are not the person we think we are! The less identified we are with our self-image and story and all the reactive feelings and contracted sensations that go with it, the more free, wakeful, authentic, spacious, and loving we are. The less we are a "someone," the freer we are to be our uniquely expressed self. In the absence of self, we find presence.

There are a number of ways to attune to this sense of presence. One that I use with others during a retreat is to invite them to settle in and rest in a sense of spacious awareness for a minute or two. It's a shortcut to tap into a small taste of presence. This practice is as simple as:

Close your eyes, take a few deep breaths, and let your attention drop down and into your body. (*Pause*)

Now effortlessly relax into a sense of spacious awareness behind your body. (*Pause*)

Rest in and as this open awareness. (*Pause*)

Give it a try right now and notice what you experience.

Most people are able to feel themselves relaxing and resting back from their ordinary thinking mind into a quiet, alert, open sense of spaciousness. After a minute or two of attuning with this open awareness, I then invite them to welcome their experience just as it is, without an agenda to fix or change it, and then simply notice what unfolds. I'll explore the power of this invitation a little later in this chapter. It strongly potentiates a natural unfolding.

There are a couple more formal methods for attuning to presence that you can practice on your own. The first brings attention to what is common in all experience, while the second is a direct attunement with the *sense* of being. Each is quite simple and straightforward.

Meditation
Discovering What Is Common in All Experience

Find a quiet place where you won't be disturbed. Sit comfortably—upright, if possible. Close your eyes; take a few slow, deep breaths; and let your attention drop down and into the core of your body. (*Pause*)

Notice your current sensory experience . . .

Sensations of touch. (*Pause*)

Of your breath and heartbeat. (*Pause*)

Of any sounds you may or can hear. (*Pause*)

Of smells. (*Pause*)

Of tastes. (*Pause*)

And of any inner visual images that may appear. (*Pause*)

Now notice any feelings or mood that you may be experiencing. (*Pause*)

Notice any thoughts that arise. These often appear as an inner narration or commentary. (*Pause*)

Now ask yourself, *What is common in all of these experiences?* (*Pause*)

Notice that awareness is present with every experience of sensation, feeling, or thought. (*Pause*)

Give your attention to this awareness. (*Pause*)

Rest in and as it. Remain here as long as you'd like.

This meditation begins as a classic mindfulness instruction by giving you space to notice the present experience, but then it turns your attention directly toward you, the apparent perceiver. The invitation here is not to *think* about awareness or *try* to cultivate it but rather to simply relax into it and know oneself as it. This practice allows us to rest back into a background awareness that is always present behind our thoughts, feelings, and sensations, like a wave subsiding into the ocean. Attention is a wave of awareness. Our egoic identity, the little you within, is a fixated point of attention that can relax back and open into its original nature as unbounded, pure awareness. It is a shift of attention from viewpoint to viewspace.

It is worth noting that here, we are taking a different direction than conventional present-centered mindfulness. Most mindfulness methods—at least at their beginning and intermediate levels—focus on training attention to be open, nonjudgmental, and present-centered. The accent is on noticing finer and finer levels of perception so the apparent object of attention, such as the breath or a body sensation, eventually dissolves. Experience is broken down into its constituent components that are seen to be in constant flux. All experience is seen to be impermanent. At very advanced stages, when the object dissolves, so too does the apparent subject. Subject and object, the perceiver and the perceived, the me and the it (or you) require each other. When one dance partner disappears, the other quickly follows.

This mindfulness approach has obvious advantages. Its benefits—such as sharpened attention, enhanced subjective well-being, improved physical health, and strengthened empathy—are well established.[2] Mindfulness does, however, pose two potential traps. First, as we try to cultivate a mental level of unconditional acceptance, it may strengthen self-judgment as we inevitably fail in this endeavor. Second, as with all progressive approaches, it will tend to cultivate a state of being, or a silent observer or witness, that remains separate. This is a particularly difficult illusion to see through. At least, it was for me. Even though I was a highly experienced meditator, I needed both of my teachers, Jean Klein and Adyashanti, to point this out and help me see through it. In truth, there is no separate witness or observer.

The approach I am introducing here is known as the direct path. It is *presence-centered* rather than present-centered. The emphasis is on seeing through the apparently localized perceiver, our conventional self-image and story, rather than the objects of perception: our thoughts, feelings, and sensations. It has its own potential pitfalls, most notably if the understanding remains on an intellectual level rather than transposing deeply into the conditioned body-mind. The mind can use any approach, progressive or direct, to avoid facing life as it is.

The other simple and direct way to attune to presence is to follow the felt-sense of "I am" inward. How and where do we detect this subtle sense? Our body knows better than our mind. Notice what your hands may do when you are talking about yourself. When you are trying to describe something that happened to you or something you really care about, your hands will often unconsciously gesture toward or touch the center of your chest: "It happened to me!" we say, with a finger pointing toward or tapping mid-chest. It's a curious phenomenon. I first began noticing it years ago when my clients talked about themselves. As a well-known public example in the US, when a person pledges allegiance to the flag, they place their hands over their physical heart. Why is this? Our deepest sense of self tends to spontaneously localize in the heart area. This is an important clue. See if it's true for you.

Meditation
Following the Sense of "I Am" Inward

Find a quiet place where you won't be disturbed. Sit comfortably—upright, if possible. Close your eyes. Take a few slow, deep breaths, and let your attention drop down and into the core of your body. (*Pause*)

Mentally repeat the thought *I am* a few times and then let it go, like dropping a pebble in a pond. (*Pause*)

Notice if there is a subtle sensation or feeling, a felt-sense, that is evoked. If so, give your attention to it. (*Pause*)

Now allow your attention to follow this felt-sense inward, as if the heart area (or wherever this sense initially localizes) is a portal opening into infinite space behind your body. (*Pause*)

Relax back and let your attention be effortlessly taken. (*Long pause*)

Rest *in* this background sense of awareness. (*Long pause*)
And now *as* this awareness. (*Long pause*)
Rest here as long as you'd like.

In this meditation, the sense of "I" is like a golden thread leading us home. It begins as the statement of a separate someone: I am this body, these thoughts and feelings, this history, an apparently solid and separate "me" that is alone in the world. Yet as we gradually follow the felt-sense of the separate self inward, it becomes less objective, less of a thing. The "I" sense opens up and feels increasingly less localized. With practice, it disappears altogether. What remains cannot be named, yet we feel ourselves at home, more "here" than ever before, even if we can't locate ourself.

When thoughts arise, as they naturally will, we can ask, *Who is experiencing this thought?* and then come back to the sense of "I." At first this inquiry takes some focused effort, but with practice, it becomes quite easy and natural. Both Ramana Maharshi and Nisargadatta Maharaj, two great twentieth-century Indian sages, recommended forms of this meditative inquiry.[3]

With this approach, the ego ("I am" in Latin) is a portal rather than an obstacle. We allow our attention to dive right into the center of the "me" and come through the other side into open, spacious awareness. As we relax into not knowing, we discover an unexpected lucid, wakeful openness. What begins as a localized sense of "me" leads to nonlocalized awareness. The emptiness of the separate self reveals the fullness of being.

These two methods are complementary. The first, "Discovering What Is Common in All Experience," relies more on discernment. The second, "Following the Sense of 'I Am' Inward," relies on felt-sensing. You may find one more accessible than the other as you begin your practice, but they both point attention toward the same background awareness. As we consciously attune with this awareness, it comes more into the foreground of our everyday experience. In time, background and foreground dissolve and awareness feels global—that is, 360 degrees all around, without an inside or outside. We are simply open.

Attuning with presence is a matter of degree, much like a dimmer switch that gradually increases the light in a room. If presence suddenly switches on in a dramatic fashion, as occasionally happens, it will almost always quickly switch off, as if an inner circuit breaker has been activated. This snapback phenomenon is quite common. It is not a mistake or failure. Our conditioned body-mind is generally not prepared for such a sudden influx of unconditioned awareness, and it will shut down and pull back from this burst of luminosity and openness. However, a positive imprint, a taste, will remain and our system will start to orient to it on a deep level. Once presence is touched, it is not forgotten. It takes time for the body-mind to acclimate to this higher vibrational level. There's no limit to how much we can embody presence. Acclimation is an ongoing, open-ended process.

The Power of Presence

Decades ago, I noticed an interesting phenomenon. After a five-day retreat with one of my teachers, the quality of my client sessions almost always markedly improved. My listening was better, my empathy was deeper and more accurate, and my sense of what was wanting to unfold was clearer. None of this was intentional; it just happened. At first, this would only last for a day, and then for several days, weeks, and months afterward. As my ability to attune with presence gradually intensified and stabilized, my client work directly benefited. This post-retreat experience with clients illustrates the spontaneous power of presence. Presence potentiates transformation. This is why I often invite my students to rest in silence and attune with spacious awareness for a minute or two before they explore their conditioning. Even this brief contact with presence frees attention from the ordinary mind so that we are able to welcome experience as it is rather than try to fix, change, or get rid of it.

Presence frees us to be intimate with our experience, to approach it with genuine curiosity and affection in order to get to know it better. This innocent approach makes all the difference. Consider how it is to be with someone who just wants to get to know you as you are rather than try to change you. We tend to relax when we feel this quality of interest and receptivity, don't we? Despite our initial ambivalence, we actually want to be heard and seen in a deep way. We want to be received with love and understanding. The same principle holds true for our inner experience. We want to feel free to show ourselves as we are—complex, unfinished, and sometimes messy—and to be received. When we feel this, we open up and a natural movement unfolds. There may be tears, trembling, and insights along the way as the body-mind starts to naturally thaw and unwind itself from its inner clench.

"Looking into the Mystery of Life from Within a Coffin"

Roland was an earnest older gentleman who had joined one of my online seminars about opening to the ground for the first time. He reported experiencing "a lot of fear, even terror" in the past few months. When I asked him what he feared, he responded that death was one aspect, but "there's more." When I inquired if he'd like to explore it a bit with me, he responded, "Yes, please."

During my online or in-person seminars and retreats, I often engage in "experiential conversations" with participants for five to ten minutes. This is almost always enough time to home in on and be with an important issue. Once we end, I encourage those I work with to continue to sit with their experience as the conversation moves on to others. The following dialogue with Roland is slightly edited for brevity.

John: Close your eyes and forget about everyone. I'll track you. Take a few deep breaths. Be open to whatever this fear is about. Let it come to you. It may be an image, a feeling, a sensation, a direct knowing. Just be receptive. No grasping. See what emerges.

Roland: During the [earlier] meditation when you asked us to allow an image, I got the image of myself lying in a coffin.

John: Okay. Good. As we were practicing last time, leave that image for a moment and rest back in your awareness. Feel space behind you, a sense of something greater—spacious, wakeful awareness. So you're just open, not trying to fix or change anything. [*One-minute pause.*] Good. From this openness, simply welcome the image of yourself in the coffin. Let it come to you in this spacious openness and notice what happens.

Roland: First of all, I seemed to be alone in this big room and then some members of my family, my siblings, are around. I am in the coffin.

John: All right, good. Stay with it.

Roland: The atmosphere is kind of friendly.

John: Interesting.

Roland: I notice now that tears are welling up behind my eyes. [*Sighs.*] I think of times recently when I was crying out, "Please don't let me either slip away from this world or be pulled away without realizing what I am in."

John: What comes to you now about what you are in?

Roland: I don't know anymore what I'm doing here, wherever here is. I just don't know what it's about. It's like I have nothing to hold on to.

John: So, that's not a bad thing to not know and to have nothing to hold on to. Stay with this for another minute, if this is okay. Just not knowing, nothing to hold on to, surrounded by [your] siblings. Let yourself be.

Roland: I notice that I am almost smiling. [*Pause*] There's an excitement, something like that. [*Pause*] In some way, things seem to have gotten brighter around me.

John: More light. I can feel that. We'll just go a little more. [*Pause*] What's happening now?

Roland: It's like a smile. I even felt something in my belly. A laugh, almost.

John: I'll share my feeling as I sit with you. It is as if you are lighting up from the inside.

Roland: [*quietly*] Yeah. [*Pause*] The words that come are "It's crazy." I don't know. It's mysterious . . . and I want to look into the mystery and be with it.

John: Beautiful. Sounds like it is happening.

Roland: Yeah.

John: So you have a beautiful meditation space here in your coffin. [*Laughs*] You are being invited. I invite you to stay here and just rest. Not holding on to anything, not knowing anything. Just open. Just allowing this mystery to unfold in you. Because you are an intimate expression of this, Roland. You are not separate from this. You are a living mystery. We all are. You are having a more intimate feel for this. Does that feel right for you?

Roland: Yeah. That feels good. Thank you.

In this touching interchange, we first found a starting point to explore his fear: the image of the coffin. I then invited Roland to step back into spacious awareness for a minute and welcome the image. A rich scene emerged with Roland in the coffin surrounded by siblings, not wanting to slip away before knowing what this life was. At first, he did not know, and there was nothing to hold on to. Where some guides might be tempted to reassure Roland that he did know and could hold on, I trusted this openness and encouraged him to stay with it. This is when a shift happened and he began to feel a sense of excitement, a brightening, an inner smile, and a laugh in his belly. I sensed that he was lighting up from the inside, and he resonated with this reflection. He was "looking into the mystery and being with it" in a direct, nonmental way. This is what he most wanted to happen before he died. His inner coffin was a portal to the natural unfolding of a mysteriously illumined sense of life.

The ordinary mind cannot facilitate this kind of spontaneous unfolding. Presence can. When we are able to attune with open, spacious awareness and welcome our experience as it is, a greater intelligence, love, and power flows through us. As a result, our mind and body unveil themselves and more fully embody the light of awareness.

5

The Sense of Inner Knowing

The more awake we are, the more we are able to
experience the whole body-mind as a literal sensing
instrument of the absolute unified self.

—Adyashanti, *The End of Your World*

Earlier I mentioned that many years ago I had a powerful inner vision of a rainbow bridge of light that spanned the earth and sky, joining the two. Over the years, as my subtle sensitivity has unfolded, the meaning of this compelling image has clarified: our body is like a bridge of light that connects our ordinary, finite life with the Infinite. Speaking poetically, our body bridges heaven and earth.

This is admittedly a strong claim. How can this dense, apparently solid object—the human body—be a luminous bridge to anything?

If we are not in touch with our body, this makes no sense at all. However, if we are deeply in touch with our body, it makes complete, visceral sense. The more in touch we are, the more sense it makes.

Making sense is an interesting phrase, isn't it? It means to understand with our senses, to arrive at some inner clarity via our capacity to see, hear, touch, taste, or smell. When someone else has drifted off into what we think is a fantasy, we wonder when they will come to their senses. A *commonsense solution* means something that is obvious and pragmatic. Different species have different sensory capacities and live within their own unique sensory environments, what the German zoologist Jakob von Uexküll called "umwelten."[1] For instance, if a dog and a bat are both put into the same dark room, each will map and inhabit a distinctive space via smell or echolocation. Their worlds will overlap and also significantly differ. In subtle ways, the same is true for humans.

In addition to our common senses, we have uncommon senses, ones that remain largely dormant until we begin to pay attention to them, most notably the ability to interoperceive, or sense into the interior of our body. The philosopher Eugene Gendlin called this "felt-sensing," which he defined as a vague, preverbal, whole-body sense of something. Gendlin, who did research with the American psychologist Carl Rogers in the 1960s, discovered that while a few people are naturally in touch with this ability, most of us can learn it with practice. He developed a method called "focusing" to do so.[2]

As we develop the ability to sense into our body beyond our breath, heartbeat, and the occasional upset stomach, we literally start to *feel* differently. We begin to get in touch with our feelings, how our emotions are experienced in our body. For example, anger will often be associated with a clench in our solar plexus and jaw; shame tends to localize as a constriction in the mid-chest and cause our face to flush; and terror makes our legs feel shaky and creates an overall freeze in the body. We may also sense how love, joy, and gratitude tend to localize mid-chest in the heart area as radiance or warmth. As we become more conscious of our feelings, the interior of our body gradually comes more online and no longer feels so dense, opaque, or distant. Instead, it feels lighter, clearer, and closer.

Meditation
Locating and Sensing Feelings

Start to notice where and how your feelings localize in your body. Sometimes they may be diffuse, and other times sharply focused. Often they happen somewhere along the midline of the trunk of your body, such as the lower belly, solar plexus, mid-chest, or throat. Notice their intensity, lightness or density, and texture. Also notice what happens as you simply allow them without any agenda to change them. If a feeling is too overwhelming, such as terror or rage, take several deep breaths and step back from it before giving it attention. We can learn to allow our feelings without becoming lost in them.

At first we may be more in touch with our feelings when we are quietly at rest. Eventually they are readily accessible under any circumstances. The more aware of them we are, the less likely we will unconsciously act them out and the more likely we will be able to skillfully express them. Being in touch with them allows us to be more intimate with ourself and with others, which is deeply fulfilling.

Of course, there are many reasons our natural sensitivity—the sensitivity we have as young children before we are heavily conditioned—is lost or dulled. In part it is cultural. Most of us live in urbanized environments estranged from nature. Further, our educational systems accent the importance of rational thought and ignore or entirely dismiss quieter, subjective ways of knowing. But most importantly, we lose or dampen our sensitivity when we have been exposed to physical or emotional abuse or neglect. When this happens, our system shuts down to avoid being overwhelmed and to stay safe.

If we do not feel sufficiently met, seen, heard, felt, held, or protected at any age, we numb ourself and check out. We learn to abandon ourselves in order to survive. Our native sensitivity, especially as children, goes underground, much like buried treasure, and there it is often forgotten. This self-uprooting and abandonment is largely an unconscious process, although sometimes as children we do consciously vow to never open up and trust again. It is just too painful and overwhelming to stay open. It is also true that some of us are just wired to be more in touch with our senses. Like anything else, there is a natural spectrum of inner sensitivity.

Recovering our sensitivity can be challenging. Opening up usually means revisiting, at least briefly, the difficult experiences that caused us to shut down in the first place—neglect, abuse, trauma, and the painful feelings and distorted thoughts they induced. Because these psychological wounds largely arose in relationship with our caretakers, they usually require corrective relationships to heal. These healing relationships may come via trustworthy friends, healthy family members, intimate partners, or trained professionals. It almost always takes time to restore trust and intimacy within oneself and with others.

Our spiritual search and discovery is strongly impacted by our psychological conditioning. While our suffering can be an incentive to more carefully examine our life and discover deeper truths about ourself, it can also make us turn to a kind of spirituality that tries to avoid our human experience—for example, by devaluing our feelings, needs, or relationships because they are not ultimately "real." This tendency is known as "spiritual bypassing," a term coined by the Buddhist psychologist John Welwood.[3] It is my understanding that spirit does not actually bypass anything, and that it is the conditioned mind that is avoidant. Regardless of what we call it, the phenomenon is quite real.

This is why I often accent the importance of honesty and vulnerability. If we are really interested in embodying spirit in our daily life, we must face our conditioning and deeply inhabit our body. If we have skeletons rattling in our closet, they will need to be exhumed and properly buried. If there are distressed inner parts, they will need to be thoroughly welcomed as they are. This book may aid in this process, as can other kinds of attuned psychotherapy and bodywork. But I want to be clear: We are not trying to resolve all of our conditioning. This is an endless and futile project, and there is no perfect or complete healing. Rather, it is a matter of inner integrity. Are we willing to bring attention to where it is called? Are we open to hearing that call?

Psychological healing and spiritual discovery are complementary movements. Each supports but does not assure the other. As we feel more resilient and coherent psychologically, we more easily access and sustain spiritual openings. As we access presence and intuit our innate wholeness, we more easily welcome our psychological conditioning. An initial spiritual awakening does not guarantee psychological maturity, as we have repeatedly seen with many spiritual teachers who act out their unresolved emotional issues with their students. Similarly, psychological maturity does not ensure a spiritual awakening. These are partially overlapping but distinctive lines of development.

The main point is that as we both heal and awaken; the body opens up and feels less like a dense, solid object and more like a field of energy. When we close our eyes, it becomes harder to detect a border between our body and the world. Our umwelt opens up.

Inquiry
Where Does the Body End?

Find a comfortable place where you won't be disturbed. Sit comfortably—upright, if possible. Take several slow, deep breaths. (*Pause*)

Allow your attention to settle down and into the core of your body. (*Pause*)

Feel the weight of your body held by whatever you are sitting upon and relax into the sense of being held. (*Pause*)

Notice the sense of space in front of your body. (*Pause*)

Then behind your body. (*Pause*)

On the left side. (*Pause*)

And on the right side now. (*Pause*)

Sense the space above your head. (*Pause*)

And below your body. (*Pause*)

Now 360 degrees all around. (*Pause*)

Notice how far this sense of space extends. (*Pause*)

Is there any end to it? (*Pause*)

Now notice the border between your body and this sense of space. (*Pause*)

Let your body dissolve into this sense of unlimited space. (*Long pause*)

Rest here as long as you'd like. When you are ready, slowly reorient to present time and place before going about your day. Notice if this sense of space is also here when you are more active.

As the sense of the body expands, we feel ourself more here. Rather than "spacing out," we actually inhabit our body more. This happens because the body's inherent nature is profoundly spacious and at ease. Under the right conditions, our body will unfold much like a fist that unclenches. (We'll explore this important theme more in chapter 14.)

Is There an Energy Body?

Just because our body may start feeling more like a field of energy, does that mean there are actually one or more "energy bodies" that comingle with our physical body? While Western scientists are very skeptical, a number of Eastern contemplative traditions would unequivocally answer yes. For instance, Indian yogic tradition describes discrete koshas, or sheaths of the body, of which the physical is the densest. Further, there are seven major energy centers, or chakras, that align from the base of the spine to the top of the head. These energy centers govern or are associated (from bottom up) with core human themes such as survival, sensuality, interpersonal power dynamics, love, creative expression, clear insight, and spiritual illumination. Further, they are part of a powerful central current called kundalini that parallels the spine.[4] Tibetan Buddhists describe a subtle body (sambhogakaya) that exists between our physical body (nirmanakaya) and our essential, spiritual body (dharmakaya). They also describe the major energy centers and a central channel of energy. Taoists describe a universal energy, or chi, field with various orbits and points associated with the physical body.

When I first began to read about these esoteric systems in my late teens, I was both intrigued and skeptical. Yet as I attended a series of rigorous six-month-long meditation courses in my twenties and also adopted a daily meditation practice, I was surprised to discover these energy centers and the central channel spontaneously emerging, even though this was not the purpose of the meditation. This energetic sensitivity further developed as I began working with clients as a counseling intern in my early thirties. Again, much to my surprise, I began to sense, via a spontaneous resonance within my body, the energy centers that were becoming active in my clients' bodies. My psychology texts and professors had certainly not prepared me for this! For example, as my clients got in touch with their grief and touched their heart areas, I could feel a less intense version of their feeling and also sense the energetic contraction deep in the mid-chest.

This spontaneous energetic unfolding was uncomfortable at times. During those early years, I would sometimes awaken at night after two hours of deep sleep and feel strong jolts of energy running down my spine. This kept me up for hours and occasionally left me exhausted during the day. The process seemed to have a life of its own as a primal life energy worked its way through various blocks in my system. I did nothing to assist or obstruct it, trusting that it needed to run its course without any conscious manipulation. Forty years later, quite thankfully, the process has quieted down from those early years of midnight rock 'n' roll.

The point of sharing this is not to emphasize my experience but rather to describe how I came to realize that our body has a subtle sense of inner knowing. Early on in this process, I found that Eugene

Gendlin's development of focusing offered a partial frame of understanding and vocabulary for what I was experiencing. It was clear that I wasn't the only one who was experiencing a wholistic way of knowing.

Inner Knowing

Gendlin's theory of felt-sensing and the practice of focusing applies to problems, situations, and people, and it is very clear that we all have a native capacity for whole-body sensing about something. As my clients would get quiet and turn their attention inward, surprising insights would unfold about the impact of their childhood conditioning or how best to navigate their current relationships and work life. But a deeper level of knowing was also arising—a knowing about their true nature.

They were having a felt-sense of who they really were. As they did, they would experience subtle bodily shifts that I could outwardly observe and sometimes inwardly sense. For example, they reported feeling more at ease, more open, more inwardly congruent, more settled, more self-accepting, and more alive. Sometimes they would sit comfortably upright rather than slouching, uncross their arms and legs, and put their feet directly on the floor. They would breathe more deeply and slowly. They would become more comfortable with verbal silence and either close their eyes during an inner search or engage in a receptive form of intimate, silent gazing interspersed with conversation. I knew these shifts and openings were very important, but I couldn't quite name what the underlying process was.

At some point it dawned on me that my clients were having a felt-sense of their inner knowing, which is distinct from having a felt-sense about *something*. They were attuning with their "being-understanding," a term that my first teacher Jean Klein used to refer to an implicit knowing of oneself that resides in the core of our being. While the body is not the source of this essential knowing, it has a sense of it. It participates in the conscious unfolding of this knowing by subtly lighting up, lining up, and opening up.

This sense of inner knowing is very relevant to both our psychological work and spiritual investigation. It helps us discern what is authentic and what is not. It also helps us avoid getting caught in self-doubt or becoming lost in the judging mind. Rather than trying to rely on our mind to discern what is true or false, we learn to listen to the subtle signals of our body. I was someone who was once plagued by self-doubt and an overactive mind, so discovering this sense of inner knowing was a godsend.

I have explored my own conditioning enough to have a fairly accurate sense of what is true and what is not in others. With others, we feel it via resonance or dissonance. If someone else is out of touch or off the mark, we can often sense this. What they express will ring true or not. For example, in chapter 3, when Janice at first concluded that she was lacking commitment, it didn't ring true for me. But when she identified the source of her resistance as fear, it did. Or when Roland reported a kind of inner lightness in the prior chapter, it felt very resonant. In both cases, my resonance was not a result of an analytic process; I didn't need to think about it.

We all experience resonance or mutual attunement to some degree. In this way, our body is like a poorly or well-tuned musical instrument. Imagine two guitars placed next to each other. If you pluck the string on one, the corresponding string will vibrate on the other. Of course, this won't happen if one of the guitars is out of tune. When we are with someone else, interpersonal resonance happens in a similar way, often below conscious awareness. If we are well attuned—that is, in touch with our own body-mind—we can feel and sense another person's experience with a certain degree of accuracy. With experience, this capacity for subtle interpersonal sensing continues to develop and refine. It's not magic; it's biology.[5] Attuning this way is like engaging in a fresh, ever-deepening conversation with our body. The more carefully we listen, the more we discover about ourself and others. Chronic knots of tension often appear before they spontaneously soften and melt. Powerful hidden dimensions of our experience reveal themselves.

To attune with others, we must first attune with ourself. For this to happen, our attention needs to drop down out of our head and into the core of our body. We must let go of our beliefs, be willing to not know, and listen with real innocence and openness. It is an art that grows with practice. We also need to be humble about our limitations and alert to the possibility of our projections. None of us is a perfectly clear or omniscient being. While we can sometimes know a lot about our or another's experience, there are limits to our understanding. We will always have blind spots.

Inquiry
Experiencing the Sense of Inner Knowing

When you open to a deep truth about yourself, such as *I am whole as I am, regardless of my flaws and limitations* or *Who I am can never be grasped by thought*, don't think about what it may mean. Instead, quietly sense and feel what's in your body. What comes to you in that moment? Let it in and allow it to be.

You are starting to attune with your inner knowing. As this strengthens, it will become an increasingly trustworthy guide for all aspects of your life. You are attuning with your inner GPS.

6

Questioning Beliefs

The primary task of any good spiritual teaching is not to
answer your questions, but to question your answers.

—Adyashanti, *The Way of Liberation*

So much of the spiritual quest is about our willingness to question
our beliefs—all of them—and unlearn what is not true. It is a
process of stripping away, an unveiling. What is it that is ultimately
unveiled? Here, the mind bows down to silence.

Jean Klein would often say that the mind must know its limits
before we can discover our real nature. I have found this to be true
and generally start my retreats accenting this insight. In order for
attention to spontaneously drop down and into the body, it must
first unhook from our ordinary thinking. The point is not to try to

stop thinking but to recognize its limits. When this happens, there is a natural letting go. Clarity—seeing the false as false—fosters an effortless surrender.

Most of us are easily lost in our thoughts. Our attention unknowingly boards a train of thought and off we go, often in a circle! For example, I was recently on a solo writing retreat in Bishop, a charming town of 3,500 people on a high desert plateau along the eastern flank of the Sierra Nevada mountains in California. A tropical storm had just crossed into Southern California for the first time since 1939, yet another harbinger of global climate disruption, and residents in Palm Springs, a desert community east of Los Angeles and three hundred miles south of me, were busy preparing for a midsummer deluge by filling sandbags to protect their businesses and homes. The outermost bands of the storm were starting to reach me. As the rain increased and the power suddenly went off, I thought about the fact that all of the local high mountain lakes were filled to the brim from the past winter's unusually heavy snowmelt. This meant the minor tributary of South Bishop Creek that ran through the backyard of the property I was on might possibly flood. If so, what should I do? I was not alarmed; I didn't really expect a crisis, but the mind briefly entertained the possibility.

Stepping back from those thoughts, I was able to observe the mind doing what it is designed to do: detect potential problems (flooding) and envision possibilities (escape). Its underlying purpose is clear: to try to know in order to have control so the body survives. In a nutshell, this is the mind's basic formula: knowing = controlling = surviving. I invite you to watch your thoughts and notice this extremely common pattern.

The human mind is an awesome evolutionary tool that also contains the seeds of its own destruction if it is not tempered by a transrational wisdom and love. The particular bizarre and destructive weather pattern I just described—a tropical storm flooding Southern California deserts—is not an accident. Canada's boreal forests, which along with the Amazon rainforests are the lungs of the planet, are constantly being ravaged by wildfires. Large chunks of Greenland and Antarctica are melting at an exponential rate. All of these events are the direct result of our unsustainable, collective addiction to fossil fuels, our stubborn denial of facts, and our collective, shortsighted egocentricity. Nuclear weapons and artificial intelligence, both products of some of humanity's finest minds, likewise threaten the existence of a vast array of species, including our own. The power of the human mind cuts both ways.

We are just as addicted, if not more, to our beliefs. We tend to mis-take them for reality, but really they are maps—more or less accurate representations and interpretations of what is real. Most thoughts are benign and do not require careful examination. Calling this trembling, leafy, white-barked object outside my window an aspen tree is not a problem. However, certain thoughts are critically important to question, especially those about who or what we think we are. They are often the lynchpins that keep the illusion of a separate self intact and fuel our collective insanity.

Thoughts, like the aspen tree, are also objects—mental ones. They are part of a running, subvocal commentary that describes our ongoing experience, seasoned with occasional unkind thoughts about ourself and others. Our thoughts shuttle between remembering the apparent past and projecting those memories into the apparent future, both of which always happen in the present moment. They weave a story about who we are and what the world is, and appear and disappear much like clouds in the sky or birdsong. Some are wispy and transient, while others are more like a thick fogbank constricting our body, coloring our mood, and obscuring our clarity. In addition to believing our thoughts, we completely overlook the silence that is between and behind them.

We humans are storytellers about what life is and who we are, individually and collectively. One of the apparently unique qualities of being human is our ability to fashion an autobiographical narrative, a story about ourself across time.[1] Whether hero or villain, we are always the star of this narrative, occupying center stage in the story of "me." Yet no matter how accurate our facts or interpretations may be, our essential nature can never be captured by thought. Our deepest nature cannot be objectified. We are not ultimately a "thing."

Who we are is prior to thought. We are literally inconceivable and unimaginable. Notice how both of these adjectives are negations. Many of the related words that contemplative traditions use to describe our true nature—*unlimited, unbounded, infinite, no one, no-thing*—also describe what we are not. Even pointing to our essential nature with words like *pure consciousness* or *awareness* can subtly mislead us, strengthening the illusion of a separate observer who stands above or behind thoughts, feelings, and sensations and witnesses them. In truth, thinking is happening, but there is no thinker. Witnessing is happening, but there is no witness.

We can never know who we are via the ordinary mind. Certainly our minds can be inspired by a deeper knowing; what is known in Sanskrit as buddhi, or the "illumined intellect." Flashes of genuine insight can take the form of metaphoric or rational thought, but the source of these flashes comes from somewhere other than the mind. The mind translates these luminous insights into words and images. Rumi, for example, was a master of this.

Given the limitation of thought, we can take refuge in not knowing. We don't know, can't know, and, most importantly, don't need to know who or what we are via thought. This inability is not a problem or personal failure. Rather, it is a fact. When the mind finally realizes that it can never grasp something beyond itself and that this is okay, the whole body-mind system experiences a deep sigh of relief. The mind no longer must pretend that it knows something that it can't. An unexpected door opens as we relax into the truth of not knowing who we are. We are open and available in a new way. We are open to openness.

The Fear of Losing Control

Before the ordinary mind surrenders to not knowing, it always puts up a fight because it fears losing control. The mind thinks, *If I'm not in control, who will run the show? Won't everything descend into chaos?* In this way, the mind is like a narcissistic politician who fears losing his or her grip on power. This grip needs to relax. This happens with insight.

There is a cautionary note here. It is vitally important that the personal will is not crushed in childhood. If this happens, a child will feel powerless and fall into despair, self-loathing, and self-distrust. This collapsed state will require that the personal will is initially repaired and empowered before the grip on control can be released. Good psychotherapy can support this. The genuine release of control comes when the limits of the personal will are seen through. It is a spontaneous surrender. As we relax our apparent control and discover that our life works as well, if not better than before, we gain trust. This is almost always a gradual process.

There are conscious and subconscious layers to our mental attempts to control. How do we go about recognizing and seeing through them? After many years of one-on-one and group practice, I've discovered a form of inquiry that effectively accesses a deeper, quieter, and more intuitive mode of knowing. The more we trust in not knowing, the easier it is to tap into this other mode.

Inquiry
What Is My Deepest Knowing about This Belief?

I've described this method in detail in chapter 7 of *The Deep Heart*, so I will only briefly touch upon it here.[2] The key to this method of investigation lies in four tenets: recognizing our core limiting beliefs, invoking our deepest knowing, being quietly receptive, and letting in what arises.

1. Recognizing our core limiting beliefs

    Core limiting beliefs deeply influence all aspects of our life—our work, relationships, self-care, and more. They are our overt, and sometimes covert, backseat drivers. Their "rules of the road" can usually be summarized in five or fewer simple words of a young child that express a belief that we are lacking and/or flawed in some deep way. Common examples are:

- I am not enough.
- I am bad.
- I am unworthy.
- I am unlovable.
- I am too damaged.

Finding the right wording is important. Since thoughts, feelings, and sensations are all connected, you can tell when you've hit upon a core limiting belief, as it comes with an emotional reaction, such as shame or fear, as well as a constriction somewhere in your body, usually in the trunk along the midline.

2. Invoking our deepest knowing: settling in, resting back, and tuning in

Once you've pinpointed your limited belief, you must let it go (imagine it like a balloon floating away, if you like), relax, let your attention first settle down and into your body, and then rest back into a sense of spacious awareness. Take a minute or two to attune. Sense into the depths of your heart area. Ask yourself, *What is my deepest knowing about [insert core belief]?* Then let the question go. Drop it like a pebble into a still pond.

3. Being quietly receptive

Don't go to your mind for an answer to this question. Be quietly receptive. Don't grasp. Take a minute to sense your body. Be open to any spontaneous felt-sense, image, word, phrase, or direct knowing. Be willing to be surprised.

4. Letting in what spontaneously arises

Once something arises, don't judge or dismiss it. Sense if it is resonant. Does it ring true? There will always be a somatic shift—a softening, enlivening, or opening—that accompanies a genuine insight. Let it in. This is where transformation happens. Our closed system is letting in the light of awareness and opening up. Breathe in the gift. Feel it in your body. Allow your body-mind to reorient to the influx of new information and energy. When an opportunity to act on the new insight/shift arises, take advantage. For example, if you're presented with a chance to be more honest or generous with a friend or partner, do so.

I invite you to stop here and take thirty or more minutes to experiment with this method. It works equally as well when you sit with an essential question, such as *Who am I, really?* It can take a little practice to get the hang of allowing versus seeking, but once you learn the basic steps, the process will become second nature. You'll learn to quietly sit with a heart-felt question, listen, and trust what unfolds.

"It's Too Painful to Be Here"

I use abbreviated versions of the "What Is My Deepest Knowing about This Belief?" inquiry when I have "experiential conversations" or dialogues with participants during online events, in-person retreats, or one-on-one meetings. It has a way of cutting to the chase.

In our first meeting online, Brad reported that he was touched by the possibility of opening to the ground, something he had once experienced when he broke his back and opened into an oceanic feeling. However, these days he reported mostly feeling a sense of despair and worthlessness because he spent most of his time trying to exit life through various unnamed "escape hatches." Our conversation quickly took a deep dive as we uncovered and questioned the core belief that it was just too painful to be here as a human being, an existential theme that I knew firsthand.

Brad: I found myself with a real mix of disparate feelings as I listened to you. One is a wash of gratitude . . . and some clarity that is really useful to me. Another side of me feels despair that I've been really good at going out the escape hatch.

John: Let's do a little experiential piece, if you're willing.

Brad: Absolutely. Totally.

John: I have the sense that there's a lot of fear in your system.

Brad: Apparently.

John: Terror, I would say. The first step is to take a few deep breaths and rest back into a sense of spacious, open awareness. [*Pause*] Often a minute is enough to touch into this. Then from this awareness, with curiosity and affection, be open to what this fear may be. [*Pause*] Maybe a word or an image or a feeling.

Brad: The word that is associated with it is a core belief of worthlessness. [*Pause*] What comes to me is that I don't want to have the responsibility to [*inaudible*] . . .

John: Responsibility to?

Brad: This is a grandiose theme—I mean the mind takes it as grandiose—for the pain of the world.

John: Okay. Is there some belief or feeling of "I don't want to be here"?

Brad: Oh yeah!

John: It's too painful. Does that touch something?

Brad: Yes [*with deep feeling*].

John: You are not alone in this feeling.

Brad: It's not my pain! [*Voice trembles.*]

John: Oh, I understand! It's not about *your* pain. It is about *the* pain here. Just allow this. Make room for it, no judgment. [*Pause*]

Brad: It has a wave form. There have been times when it felt like I came to some deeper joy in the midst of it, but that's been awhile.

John: So this is really good. It's part of self-honesty and vulnerability to be able to touch and recognize it. This is an existential issue. Begin to ask yourself, "What is my deepest knowing about this now?" Ask yourself and then let the question go, be quiet. Notice what happens. [*Pause*]

Brad: It's really okay on some level; it's really deeply okay. [*Voice trembles.*]

John: Good. So, let this in, okay? It's really okay on some deeper level. Letting it in is very important.

Brad: Yeah. It's not real easy. [*Voice trembles.*]

John: Breathe.

Brad: I don't know why it's hard to let in.

John: So this is your edge, Brad: letting in this knowing of what's true now. This will be something for you to sit with in a very innocent, patient, and kind way. For me, this is the infusion of the light of awareness into the density of our conditioning. This is exactly what we are here for. Not to be elsewhere but to know that despite this great suffering, this is where I want and need to be. We can circle around later to see how you're doing.

Brad: That sounds good, John. Thank you.

John: [*to the larger group*] The issue that Brad raised—not wanting to be here—is definitely something I've experienced in myself. I remember when it arose about twenty-five years ago. I was shocked to see there was this avoidant tendency. [There was] an overly transcendent orientation to my spiritual path. It was a real sobering insight.

[At that time] I also realized that whatever we resist persists. I was locking myself in with my resistance. That was a really big insight in terms of turning even more directly toward my experience. The theme of not wanting to be here fuels the spiritual path for many of us, or at least some of us. That's been true for me. It was important to see this tendency to avoid, subtly and not so subtly, the challenge of being human.

Brad was describing a profound existential theme: the challenge of opening to the collective suffering of being human. His challenge wasn't about being with *his* pain; it was about being with *our* pain. No wonder he'd sought out "escape hatches" and then judged himself as being worthless for doing so.

In this exchange, I zeroed in on Brad's fear because it felt primary to me. His feelings of despair and worthlessness seemed secondary, resulting from his avoidance of this fear. Yet it quickly became obvious that Brad was not avoiding his personal pain. Instead, he was avoiding the *collective* pain of humanity. Brad seemed clear that it was not his responsibility to bear this collective pain: "It's not my pain!" It's possible that his strong assertion may have been a defense against an underlying feeling that he was responsible; however, I was struck by his clarity. This felt important to validate.

Despite his clarity that the pain was not his, he was terrified of it. It seemed to me that his underlying belief was that it was just too painful to be here as a human being. When I suggested this, he immediately agreed, opening to another level of vulnerability. I recognized this belief because it was one I had unknowingly carried and had been shocked to uncover some years before. In addition to my love of truth, my spiritual quest had been partially fueled by a desire to escape the human condition.

As soon as Brad questioned his belief that it was too painful to be here, he realized that on some level it was really deeply okay. His inner knowing was clear. Yet when I invited him to let in this knowing, it wasn't easy. Something else needed to clarify before this could happen. If we had more time, I suspect we would have gotten to it, but since I was working with a large group, I needed to move on. That reluctance to accept was his edge, and I encouraged him to stay with it and allow his inner knowing to coexist with his fear. This was okay with him. A door had begun to open.

It is one thing to sense and avoid our personal suffering. It is another to avoid the collective suffering of humanity. The more we open our hearts, the more we feel both of them. It can feel especially overwhelming to open to this collective suffering if we believe we must somehow hold it by ourself. The good news is we don't have to hold it alone. There is something greater that holds the collective suffering of humanity. I like to call it the Great Heart; others call it the Divine Mother or a field of unconditional loving awareness. Whatever we call it, it is beyond the ordinary mind.

Part 2

THE DESCENT

O nce we are suitably equipped with a map and inner resources, we are ready for a deep dive. Sometimes, however, a crisis knocks us off our feet and we find ourselves tumbling into a dark abyss completely unprepared. In either case, there is a descent. Whether pulled by our suffering or pushed by the intuition that there is greater depth to life, we feel our attention drawn down and in. As these depths consciously unfold, it can feel like our center of gravity is deepening. The ground feels closer and more palpable.

Yet almost always, there will be periods when we feel more disoriented and ungrounded, especially as we begin to encounter and see through our false ground, that which we have stood upon and mistook to be real and solid. During this phase, the fear of letting go and losing control can be quite strong. This disorientation is a prelude to a far deeper reorientation as we come into alignment with the truth of our being.

7

Seeing Through False Ground

To know what you are, you must first
investigate and know what you are not.

—Nisargadatta Maharaj, *I Am That*

There are different levels of being grounded. For instance, when we
are in touch with our body and the earth, we are more physically
grounded; we love being in nature and feel at ease in our body. We
also can be grounded mentally, emotionally, and energetically so that
we think, feel, and subtly sense clearly. All of these relative ways of
grounding allow us to be in touch with our precious present-centered
experience, yet our deepest ground unfolds when we discover our
true nature as open, loving awareness. Reality, relative or absolute, is
inherently grounding. However, almost all of us unknowingly stand

upon a false ground that veils our deepest ground. Seeing through our false ground allows the true ground to spontaneously emerge. We saw examples of this in the prior chapters with Janice, Roland, and Brad. As each of them relaxed into presence and opened to their deepest knowing, they experienced an upwelling of deeply felt insight that began to infuse longstanding, rigid inner stances. Their inner experience spontaneously opened, softened, melted, unwound, and illuminated. In each case, something tightly held began to release.

This tightly held inner grip is our false ground, and its hallmark is contraction, a largely unconscious attempt to be safe by pulling in and holding back. I think of it as a core contraction. Most of us are not directly aware of it until we start to deeply relax. When we do, we can sense what is unable or unwilling to relax within us. Mostly we know this core contraction by its side effects: feeling chronically ill at ease, anxious, driven, and disconnected. There are different levels to this false ground that correspond to our unique psychological conditioning, but we all share an existential level that arises from our commonsense experience of being a separate self. Each of us inherently resists reality and tries to hold onto illusion in a unique way. We then identify with and attach to this form of self-holding.

We are strangely devoted to this frozen, contracted state. This was one of the most surprising phenomena I encountered as a new therapist. People cling to their suffering, much like a child who clings to a dysfunctional parent. We prefer a known suffering to an unknown openness—*I've always felt this inner contraction, so this must be who I really am.* On some level we construct an inner prison cell and conclude that it is our home, miserable as it is. We then mistake ourself as a prisoner. Yet the bars of our prison are made of ice, not steel. Although they may initially feel impenetrably solid, they can soften and melt. As they do, a truer ground reveals itself. Further, the back of our self-constructed prison cell is always open. When we rest back into spacious awareness, we can immediately sense our freedom. The ability to rest back and see our apparent prison for what it is allows its tight grip to release. The sense of space invites (but does not assure) a letting go.

While we can sense false ground anywhere in our body, it tends to localize along the midline, from the top of the head to the base of the spine. We feel it as a persistent knot of tension or freeze in the forehead, back of the head, throat, heart area, solar plexus, lower belly, or base of the spine. We can also sense it as a constriction along the entire vertical core of our body. It affects how we think about, feel, and sense our self, others, and life in general. When we are in the grip of our false ground, we are close-minded, close-hearted, and close-bodied. Our attention is fixated and veiled. Most of us take this closed way of being as normal and natural. I did for many years, until it gradually released.

False ground in the area of the head corresponds with rigid thinking and dogmatically held beliefs, some of which are subconscious. It's like wearing a medieval war helmet with a narrow viewing slot. I have found that subconscious limiting beliefs tend to localize at the back of the head in the area of the occipital lobe, whereas ones that are conscious tend to localize in the prefrontal cortex—the forehead. Because our psychological field of vision is constricted and distorted with the false ground, we are easily blindsided by unexpected events and, as a result, feel vulnerable and defensive. Letting go of such a rigid way of seeing can be disorienting at first, as if we have wandered out of a dark cave into the bright sunlight.

Inquiry
How Does It Feel to Let Go of a Core Limiting Belief?

Reflect on a time when you released a core limiting belief about yourself, others, or life. What did you experience? How did you feel in your body?

A chronic constriction or freeze in either the front or back of the throat area usually corresponds to us holding back our authentic self-expression, almost always because it did not feel safe to do so when we were a child. Sometimes tears were choked back, leading to unexpressed grief. Sometimes there was an inner protest, like *No! Stop! I don't want this!* when it felt like we couldn't set a healthy boundary. Sometimes we were forced to hold an unwanted secret. And sometimes we were afraid or ashamed to sing our song or tell our deepest truth because we didn't believe that anyone wanted to hear it or we thought we would be punished or humiliated if we did. Often the throat is a "bottleneck" that prevents the natural movement of energy welling up from the heart area or somewhere lower in the body and moving out into the world.

The depths of the heart area at mid-chest go into a deep freeze when we feel unloved and unlovable. When this happens very early on, the feelings of being utterly alone and disconnected are so overwhelming and intolerable that the core of the heart area shuts down. It is as if a circuit breaker is thrown to prevent total dysregulation. From time to time, I have touched this place with those of my clients and students who never really bonded with their primary caretakers or who lost them very early on. It is a state of living hell—the hell of separation.

When this level of contraction occurs, there is a deep withdrawal from life. It can feel as if our spirit dies. In fact, the most tender, most sensitive, and most innocent part of our human nature withdraws into a tight ball and buries itself deep into the psyche. I'm sure you have experienced some form of this shock as an adult when you withdrew emotionally and energetically from another person in order not to be hurt. The impact is magnified manyfold when we are infants who are totally dependent on our caretakers. When we are abandoned at such a primal level, we also unconsciously abandon ourself because it is just too painful to bear our inner experience. We must split ourself off from our essential core in order to survive. Although this happens prior to any thoughts or words, a primitive self/worldview forms of being an unwanted self in a hostile or uncaring world.

The results of this kind of conditioning are profound. Most of us who experience this compensate and soldier forward using our talents and doing our best, but we feel a gnawing sense of lack in our heart along with a nameless grief. We become overcontrolling and critical of ourself and others. We have difficulty forming close bonds or feeling at ease in relationships. Real human intimacy feels out of reach. We feel estranged and alienated from ordinary life. Often there is an inner dread and despair. We do not trust ourself, others, or life.

It is very hard to contact this level by ourself. Almost always, it takes the attuned love and care of someone else to reach it. Layers of defense must first relax and soften. Interestingly, both parties can feel when contact is made at this core level of the heart. It can be quite a surprise for a distressed person to experience the attuned presence of another person in this zone of abject aloneness. This in itself is healing. Once we feel met in an attuned way on this level, we can more easily reconnect with this abandoned self. When someone else is able to attune with and tolerate our long split-off and buried experience, we learn to do the same. A deep inner freeze starts to thaw.

Although I am describing the effects from the most extreme cases of neglect or abuse, you likely have experienced some level of this in your life. In terms of early attachment or bonding styles, most of us have not experienced fully secure attachments with our primary caretakers. (I talk about two ways to assess this in my prior books.)[1] Most parents are not fully prompt, appropriate, and consistent in their parenting, and as a result, most of us feel some degree of anxiety. Further, many of us have experienced heartbreaking losses of significant others through death or breakups. All of these disappointments, ruptures, and losses impact the heart area and cause us to be more guarded as we consider sharing the depths of our heart with someone else.

Though the goal here is to soften and thaw, it is still important to be discerning about who we open our heart to. Some people are not trustworthy and will unconsciously and sometimes purposefully manipulate our emotional sensitivity for their own ends. Of course, the deepest, impersonal level of the heart cannot be hurt, but the more personal and human levels can be. It is a joy to find kindred spirits who can attune with and share all of these dimensions of the heart. We will not open our heart to others, certainly not for long, unless we feel safe. If we fear that we'll be judged, shamed, rejected, or abandoned, we will hold back. This complex assessment is heavily influenced by our early attachment style that sets a strong template for all of our adult relationships with friends and lovers.

Inquiry
Is It Safe to Open My Heart to Others?

Close your eyes, take a few deep breaths, and allow your attention to settle down and into the core of your body. (*Pause*)

Bring your attention to the heart area at mid-chest. (*Pause*)

Imagine that you can breathe directly into the heart area so each breath takes your attention more deeply in and back. (*Pause*)

Ask yourself, *Is it safe to open my heart to others?* Drop in the question and let it go. Don't go to your mind for an answer. Be open to any form of response—a felt-sense, image, word, or a direct knowing. (*Pause*)

Notice what comes to you. Let it in. (*Pause*)

Notice, too, if any other areas of the body respond to this inquiry.

As with other inquiries, be sure to let in your insights. Breathe and notice how they impact your body. This is how transformation happens.

I am spending some time describing this heart-centered contraction because it is one of the main locations of our false ground. We are very sensitive beings, and the heart area is a primary center of our feeling, sensing, and knowing. If you pay careful attention to the interior sensations of your body as you navigate relationships, you'll notice that contractions in the heart area are often, although not always, accompanied by contractions in the solar plexus and in the pelvic bowl at the base of the spine.

If the heart area (at mid-chest) feels threatened, we will instinctively try to control ourself or another (at the solar plexus) in order to be safe (at the base of the spine). These three centers make up an interrelated defense system that frequently gets activated as we navigate new or difficult interpersonal relationships. I invite you to pay attention to this dynamic, especially when you are in actual or potential intimacy or conflict with someone.

The area of the solar plexus (just below the diaphragm) governs interpersonal power dynamics and as such clenches when we try to overcontrol ourself or others, usually as an attempt to stay safe. When this happens, it may feel like we have a tight fist in our belly. Most people can sense this more easily than the contraction at the base of the spine, though these two areas are very closely related. After all, most perceived threats to our safety in modern times come in relationship to other people rather than the natural environment, like cave bears and woolly mammoths (more on this in the next chapter).

The strongest bastion of false ground lies, appropriately enough, at the base of the spine. Almost always, this is the most locked-down area of the body. It is located at the very bottom of the hara, or belly— the sub-hara. For unknown reasons, I have a particular sensitivity to this area that functions like a subtle radar. When someone goes into survival fear, I can sense it, much like one of those special airplanes that track hurricanes. This terror is more than ordinary fear; we can feel the difference.

Terror is extreme fear that impacts the body in a distinctive way by inducing a primal freeze. When we are terrified, the subtle body contracts, particularly at the base of the spine, and attention shoots up through the torso into the head, creating a state of hypervigilance. Our eyes unconsciously scan for danger. Our attention pulls up and out of our body because it does not feel safe. Terror induces dissociation. When we are terrified, we uproot ourself from the ground, losing connection with both the earth and our body. Subjectively it feels like the rug has been pulled out from under us. We feel deeply disoriented, ungrounded, and uprooted. We may feel subtly dizzy and sense a shakiness in our legs, as if we have nothing to stand upon or support us. If we feel this for too long, especially as children, the world no longer feels like a safe place and instead feels menacing or hostile. This is the felt worldview of a chronically neglected, abandoned, or abused child.

When terror is pronounced, there is a cascade of physiological reactions, including an adrenaline rush, rapid heart rate, and shortness of breath, along with subjective feelings of intense anxiety. The body prepares to fight, flee, or freeze in order to deal with the perceived threat. For the most part, we tend to freeze or inwardly flee, especially when we are little.

Whereas most mammals are able to naturally release the impacts of this hyperactivation and regulate themselves, we modern humans tend to store it in our bodies and remain dysregulated.[2] These unmetabolized residues manifest as post-traumatic stress. The stronger and more frequent the traumas are, the deeper the cumulative impact is on all aspects of an individual's life[3] as well as on a community—for example, one that has experienced genocide, war, or a deadly pandemic.[4]

While the well-documented effects of trauma impact all areas of human functioning, I am accenting the subjective sense of frozen ground. When this frozen ground is chronic, it becomes our false ground. On some level, we take it as a deep truth about who we are and how the world is. We then cling to it as something solid. By doing so, we take our stand upon an illusion.

The False Ground of the Separate Self

So far I've been describing the sense of false ground that arises from our family of origin. We can think of this as our personal psychological layer. Another layer of false ground arises as we face various existential challenges—entering into intimate relationships, finding meaningful work, being personally authentic, opening to life and death, and discovering our true nature, to name a few.

As part of this challenge, all of us must navigate our survival fear regardless of how benign our upbringing seemingly was. No one escapes this; we must all deal with the loss of loved ones, illness, aging, mental and physical disability, and death. There is a word that encompasses all of these phenomena: *impermanence*. Everything comes and goes, including the experience of being a separate self.

The sense that I am inside this body somewhere (don't ask me where exactly), you are over there in a different body, and there is a world "out there" separate from the "me in here" is taken for granted. It's obvious that there is a subject (me) and an object (you or it), isn't it? Few of us question this commonsense experience. However, it happens not to be true, and something in us—call it heart-wisdom—knows this.

Certainly there are distinctive body-minds and personalities. We each have a separate form and signature vibration, but we are not limited to these unique forms. We are not *just* this form. To use a classic metaphor, we are not only a wave; we are also the ocean from which the wave arises and into which the wave subsides. We are both formed and formless, finite and infinite.

As discrete, finite beings, we are rooted in the infinite. We are individual beings who are grounded in universal being. We have intuitions of this from time to time when we catch a glimpse or have the feeling of being part of something much greater. We yearn for this wholeness, but we also fear it. Why? We fear losing our self.

"I'm Afraid to Lose Myself"

A few days ago, I met with Nora for our first one-on-one spiritual mentoring session. She shared that she had been a lover of God since she was a young girl and had a very sweet, devotional I-Thou relationship with the divine as an adult. She was very familiar with nondual teachings, but she did not want to lose this connection with God. She also sensed that there was another step she was afraid to take.

John: What do you fear?
Nora: [*long pause*] I'm afraid to lose myself.

I could sense a small contraction at the back of her heart and at the base of her spine as she shared this.

John: What is your deepest knowing about this? What's the truth? Don't think about it. Let it come to you.

She closed her eyes and settled into a state of deep receptivity. After a few minutes, she spoke.

Nora: Something in me knows that it's not true. I can't lose myself. Who I am can never be lost. Everything is opening up. I know that I am everything.

She smiled with delight and opened her brightly shining eyes.

Nora: Oh, my gosh!
John: How about, "Oh, my God!" [*Laughs*]
Nora: *Yes.* Oh, my God! [*Pause*] There is a sense of the infinite.
John: Both infinite and intimate.
Nora: That would be a great book title! [*Laughs*]

As this opening continued, Nora felt it move down through her whole body. I reflected that this was a "waking down" of awareness, which was resonant for her. She reported that prior openings had always been around the head or the heart area, but this included the lower half of her body for the first time. She could feel it entering her belly, pelvis, legs, and feet, all of which were subtly vibrating. I encouraged her to simply allow this natural movement to continue down through her body and deep underground.

Nora: It's as if I have roots that are spreading out beneath me.

She motioned with her hands spreading outward below her.

John: It's like being a great tree, isn't it? The branches spread out high above and the roots spread out far below, and then it is as if the branches and the roots join. Form and formless are not different.

Nora: Form and formless are not different. My mind can't grasp this, but somehow I know that it's true. I need to let this in.

At the end of the session, Nora sat astonished and grateful, basking in the sense of radiant wholeness. I explained that often the body-mind needs to acclimate and orient to this new degree of openness, and that sometimes there might be a snapback where some resistance in the body-mind arises.

Nora: Inner acclimation, yes. It's like how our eyes have to adjust when we step outside after being in a dark room.

In terms of future steps, I told her she was being worked on and that it was enough to sit quietly with this benevolent infusion of awareness during her morning meditations, to let it in and let herself know what she knew.

John: It's an inner *Yes, Thy will be done.*

Nora: I don't have to do anything, just let it in? And for all these years I thought I was the one who had to work on myself!

John: That's just a bit of innocent confusion. It is enough to see what isn't true.

Several months later, Nora and I had a second session. She reported continuing to have some access to spacious awareness; however, a conflict with a coworker had threatened her job and stirred up a childhood fear of being alone and unable to care for herself. As we explored her experience, she could feel a subtle terror of being groundless. As she welcomed this experience into presence, as I have described in prior chapters, the clench began to release and she realized that some very young part of her was beginning to feel held. As this psychological layer of gripping eased, a deeper existential layer of feeling separate from the whole of life and trying to clench to be safe emerged. As this tension released, her attention spontaneously shifted to her lower belly, where she felt collected and settled. She felt as if she was taking her inner seat in a simple and natural way.

Our first session was admittedly unusual, while the second, where Nora's deep survival fear had been triggered, was more typical. Reading accounts like this, you might think, *That kind of opening has never happened and will never happen to me*. I encourage you to see this thought *as a thought* and let it go. Keep an open mind. Like Nora, you may find yourself unexpectedly opening to your wholeness one day and spontaneously finding your inner seat.

Nora had a strong spiritual inclination her whole life, had been exposed to many profound teachings, and had attended many retreats. She was ripe for this revelation and needed a little help to see through a small veil that obscured her true nature. Once she did, much to her surprise, there was a very rapid and natural unfolding. She had sensed that she was on the edge of an opening; she had not realized how close she actually was. Later, she was triggered by a conflict with a colleague that allowed her to uncover and welcome more of her undigested conditioning. This led to an even more stable sense of spacious awareness. In my experience, this process of deepening and stabilizing is open-ended. Life offers us many opportunities to practice!

In both sessions, Nora clearly saw the false as false. This sudden clear seeing arose from her depths in response to her heartfelt inquiry. This was the key that unlocked this recognition. In each case, when she saw through her underlying beliefs—first that she could lose herself, second that she was not held, and finally that she was fundamentally separate—the truth effortlessly emerged. Her false ground dissolved and her true ground naturally unfolded.

The Power of Seeing Through the False

It is enough to simply see the false as false. As Nisargadatta Maharaj, the luminous-eyed sage and former bidi salesman from Mumbai, India, put it, "To know what you are, you first must investigate and know what you are not."[5] Despite appearances, we are not a separate self. When we believe we are essentially separate, we take our stand upon false ground. Despite our best efforts to distract and numb ourselves, on some level we know we are skating on thin ice that could collapse at any moment. No wonder many of us, no matter how well-adjusted and financially secure, feel an underlying anxiety that is not just about our impending physical death.

Our path to truth comes by seeing the false as false. This clarity does not come from the ordinary mind. It includes reason but is not bound by it. It is a transrational insight that wells up from the depths of our being when there is an earnest inquiry. Our love for the truth comes from the truth. This is not the "truth" of some belief system or ideology. It is not a truth that can be asserted or denied. It is the truth of our being. This light of awareness, this openness, this wholeness is always right here, quietly awaiting our conscious recognition.

Inquiry
What Is the Lynchpin of My False Ground?

Once you have checked in about whether you really want to know the truth and have found an honest "yes," find a quiet place where you won't be disturbed, sit comfortably, close your eyes, and take a few slow, deep breaths. (*Pause*)

Then ask yourself, *What is the lynchpin of my false ground? What is the feeling or belief that is holding my sense of being a separate self together?* Then let the question go and don't think about it. Be quiet and receptive. (*Pause*)

If something spontaneously arises, ask yourself, *What is my deepest knowing about this? What is the truth?* Again, be quiet and receptive. (*Pause*)

Let in whatever arises. Let yourself know what you know. Notice what happens as you do. Does your sense of the ground shift in any way?

If nothing specific arises during this inquiry, notice if you are spontaneously drawn to this question on another occasion. It may take another form or be more meaningful at another time.

8

The Knot in the Belly

The level of the gut is our most existential sense of
self. It's that part of ourselves where there is a core
type of grasping—a grasping at our root.

—Adyashanti, *The End of Your World*

Have you ever experienced an uncomfortable knot of tension in
your gut? I suspect everyone has. Even though it has greatly
reduced over the years, I've carried tension there for as long as I can
remember. When I entered psychotherapy in my early thirties, I discovered that most of it originated from my relationship with my mother.
While she was generally very loving, fair-minded, and consistent with
me, she also had high standards and experienced difficulty expressing strong emotions, especially anger. She had been conditioned to

control herself and others by subtly shaming and withdrawing her affection. I unconsciously reacted to this form of control as a child by suppressing my feelings and holding my breath.

As a teenager I rebelled against her subtle regimen of control. However, when I was an adult and learned more about her childhood, I understood and felt compassion for how she learned to cope with the death of her mother when she was eight years old and her subsequent sense of being unwanted and unloved by her stepmother. It was unsafe for her to express her grief and resentment. She needed to repress her experience to survive and retain the connection with her father, whom she loved.

Naturally she imported this conditioning into her parenting style. As a sensitive boy, I could easily feel her disapproval. I could see it in her hardened gaze and hear it in her cooler tone of voice when I had broken some rule. The unconscious messaging was clear: if I misbehaved, she would withdraw her love. As a result, I learned to control myself, especially my anger, by holding my breath and tightening my gut. I feared making a misstep that might trigger her disapproval. This gradually created chronic tension in my diaphragm and a strong knot in my solar plexus area. I was trying to keep a grip on myself in order to stay connected with her. It took decades for this old pattern of fearful self-control to soften and unwind. Can you relate?

My conditioning was fairly benign compared with many of my former clients and current students who have had to navigate far more challenging circumstances, like raging, highly critical, or absent fathers; severely depressed, disconnected, or critical mothers; deaths of beloved parents or siblings; verbal and physical abuse; racism; or shaming and shunning for being LGBTQIA+. The list is long. In all of these instances, we learn to shut down and pull in to protect ourselves, burying our precious sensitivity. We then try to numb or distract ourself. Sometimes we lash out in rage or turn our anger against ourself, which also tends to localize in the solar plexus.

Psychological Fear and Existential Terror

There is a subtle somatic link between our psychological anxiety and our existential terror. If we explore our social anxieties deeply, they always lead to the terror of annihilation. You can prove this to be true by simply asking, *And then what will happen?* several times. For instance, if you feel anxious about setting a boundary, sharing a feeling, or telling an uncomfortable truth to someone, ask yourself what you fear might happen. Often the first response will be something like, *I'll be attacked and/or rejected.* If you ask again, another layer arises: *I'll be all alone.* On a subsequent inquiry, you may encounter something like, *I'll be abandoned and left out on the streets to die.* It doesn't take much probing to uncover this link. Survival terror underlies our social anxiety because we innately fear being banished from the tribe. For a child, this would mean certain death. Even though as an adult we can see that this is completely irrational, it continues to operate on a deep level, affecting all of our relationships.

On an energetic level, this powerful link between psychological and existential fear happens between the solar plexus and the base of the spine, the seat of our deep inner need for safety. The inner formula is control = safety. If I can successfully navigate my relationships with others, I'll survive. This pattern tends to localize as a simultaneous clench in the solar plexus and at the base of the spine. It is easier to sense this tension in the gut than in the pelvic bowl, where it tends to be less conscious and harder to access.

The belly in general and the area of the solar plexus in particular make up our underground control center. The image of a submarine with a long periscope comes to mind. This is where the "controller"— that part of the psyche that is trying to keep everything under control—dwells. The controller likes to stay hidden; it feels safer managing everything out of sight. Remember Janice's secret guardian in chapter 3? Being exposed might jeopardize its crucial mission to ensure survival. Sometimes this inner guardian continues like a frozen sentinel long after the rest of our body-mind system has matured, much like the Japanese soldier who continued to survive in the jungles of the Philippines thirty years after the end of World War II.[1]

This controller is a slightly older child part whose adaptation style is deeply shaped by its family of origin. Certain systems of inner parts work, such as Internal Family Systems or Voice Dialogue, have developed skillful ways to evoke and work with this and other parts.[2] Often we need to secure the controller's permission in order to access more vulnerable parts, feelings, and needs. One of the controller's main jobs is to defend against feeling too much, particularly the feeling of powerlessness. This is one of the hardest feelings to tolerate, and as such, it is often accompanied by rage. The two are closely related. Since rage can be very destructive, it is tightly controlled. Yet in its core, there is an impulse to protect our own or another's life. Only when the raw power of rage is tempered with understanding and compassion can it transform into a benevolent, creative force instead.

When we encounter circumstances that are beyond our control, such as our own illness or the death of a loved one, we feel powerless and are forced to our knees. These difficult circumstances, while painful, are often fruitful opportunities for us to practice letting go of our illusory control and begin discovering a different operating system.

Limits of Control

While control is useful, its scope is quite limited. Any biological system needs to self-regulate in order to maintain homeostasis and survive. It is natural and healthy to do so. At the same time, as humans, we never really know what is going to happen next, including our next thought. We are constantly surprised by what life brings—sometimes it's roses, and other times, thorns. Who among us knows the precise time or circumstances of our death?

But how much control do we actually need? Consider the metaphor of driving a car. If we are not in a self-driving car, we will need to keep our hands on the steering wheel to avoid running a light, going off the road, or hitting another vehicle. Taking our hands off the wheel or closing our eyes for more than a few seconds could quickly lead to a fatal accident. On the other hand, if we are hypervigilant and hold the wheel in a death grip, we are also an unsafe driver. Ideally we are relaxed and as alert as possible while navigating the busy road of life.

This metaphor has a problem, though. If our body is like a car, is there actually a discrete driver in charge? If so, I invite you to try to find one! Who or what is actually "driving" this body-mind? Where is the "me"? The conscious mind that largely localizes in the prefrontal cortex assumes that it is the driver, yet it is obvious that some of our most important physiological functions, such as breathing and digestion, are going on beneath conscious awareness. Then there's our conditioning.

Our choices are deeply influenced by both our conditioning and genetics. Why is it that so many criminals have traumatic childhoods? And how is it that identical twins, who have been separated at birth and raised in different families, can have many of the same peculiar habits and preferences? For example, there is the remarkable case of the identical twins Jim Spring and Jim Lewis who were separated at birth and raised by different families about forty miles apart in Ohio. When they were reunited at age thirty-nine, they discovered that they both

> got terrible migraines, bit their nails, smoked Salem cigarettes, drove light-blue Chevrolets, did poorly in spelling and math, and had worked at McDonald's and as part-time deputy sheriffs. But the weirdest part was that one of the Jim twins had named his first son James Alan. The other had named his first son James Allan. Both had named their pet dogs Toy. Both had also married women named Linda—then they got divorced, and both married women named Betty.[3]

While these kinds of coincidences are exceptional, even for identical twins raised apart, it clearly demonstrates how influential our genes can be. Yet genes are probabilistic, not deterministic. They don't stand alone; they are also affected by our environment. The field of epigenetics studies how our behavior—including diet, exercise, or sleep—along with circumstances, such illness or trauma, can inhibit or enhance the expression of particular genes. The interactive cycle between genes and the environment is extraordinarily complex and difficult to decode.[4] Further, as social and biological beings, our actions are informed by an unfathomable web of conditioning that stretches back to the origins of life on earth and beyond. So, how much conscious control of our life do we actually have? Not as much as we think. And who or what is in control? That's a very interesting question! Let's explore this experientially.

Releasing the Knot of Control

Releasing the knot of tension in the belly directly corresponds with letting go of our attempt to *overcontrol* ourselves and others. Unwinding this tension requires that we let go of the illusion that we can control what we can't—ourselves, others, and life itself. This grip is both somatic and cognitive. On a somatic level we can welcome the knot in the belly from spacious presence without trying to fix or change it. Instead, we can be curious and affectionate with it in order to get to know it better, even if the discomfort lasts for the rest of our life. When we stop resisting our resistance, we enter into a spacious relationship with it. We let ourself innocently be with the contraction without an agenda. Sometimes this willingness to just be with the knot, rather than subtly trying to control it, allows it to immediately soften and unwind.

Often, however, we will also need to identify the belief that accompanies the knot. Usually this belief centers around the fear of losing control: "If I lose control, something terrible will happen." Because this attempt at self-control is always associated with an inner grip, I like to pose the question: "What happens if you lose your grip on yourself?" When we work with this question on retreats, it is extremely evocative. I invite you to give it a try.

Inquiry
What Happens If I Lose My Grip on Myself?

Find a place where you won't be disturbed for a few minutes and sit comfortably upright, if possible. Close your eyes, and take several deep, slow breaths. (*Pause*)

Let your attention drop down and into the core of your body. (*Pause*)

Bring your attention to the heart area, the center of your chest. (*Pause*)

Now bring your attention to your solar plexus. (*Pause*)

Ask yourself, *What happens if I lose my grip on myself? What is my deepest knowing about this?* (*Pause*)

Don't think about it. A response can come as a felt-sense, an image, a word, or a silent knowing. Be quiet and receptive. Be willing to be surprised. (*Long pause*)

Let in whatever comes. (*Long pause*)

Notice how it acts on you. (*Long pause*) (If nothing arises, don't be concerned. You may find a version of this inquiry that is more resonant for you, or it simply may not be a relevant or important question to ponder at this time.)

In my experience, the area of the solar plexus has multiple layers similar to the heart area. Sometimes it will be enough to simply sense into the knot of tension or inquire into its related belief a few times for it to completely unwind. More commonly, it unwinds or melts in progressive stages. As we go deeper, we encounter earlier layers of conditioning. Deeper contractions generally take more time to release. This release usually feels like an easing, softening, unwinding, or melting. Tension relaxes and opens, allowing more energy, a sense of flow, and a feeling of connection with the rest of the body. Some people report a feeling of the belly coming into alignment with the pelvis, the heart area, or both.

The diaphragm and the solar plexus seem to be the most common areas where people feel an internal separation, as if the top half of their body has been severed from the lower half by a solid wall. The lower half of the body tends to feel numb or frozen, like an uninhabited wasteland. As the lower part comes into connection and alignment through introspection, felt-sensing, and honest questioning, there is a sense of deep integration and grounding.

In addition to the vertical integration of upper and lower halves of the body, people report sensing more space and openness in front of and behind the area of the solar plexus when that tension is allowed to melt away. It can feel as if a big space opens up behind the solar plexus from which a different kind of energy radiates through us. This is often accompanied by a sense of greater non-personal power, a power that does not belong to or refer to anyone.

This opening up of space behind the solar plexus marks a shift from the personal to the transpersonal will. The sense of agency changes. Rather than becoming more willful, we become more willing. *Willfulness transmutes into willingness.* This willingness is based on a sense of surrender and trust in something far deeper and greater than the "little me." It is the release from egocentric action and an opening to being in spontaneous service to the greater whole. The spiritual leader and social activist Mahatma Gandhi knew this power firsthand and gave it a special name: satyagraha, or truth force. It was the nonviolent force that helped liberate India from the stifling and sometimes violent grip of British colonialism. Inspired by Gandhi, Martin Luther King Jr. invoked this same force to propel the civil rights movement in the United States in the 1960s.

My best teaching comes when I trust this other mode of doing. I know I don't have to figure everything out in advance before I speak or somehow do "it" perfectly—whatever "it" may be. Rather, I trust in silence, stillness, and not knowing. The words come out of the silence. The action comes out of the stillness. There is an openness, an availability, that brings an aliveness, freshness, and sense of in-the-moment discovery as I share. I am sure that many of you have experienced this from time to time. Athletes call it a flow state.

Who or what is the "doer" when this happens? There is no one around to take credit for the action. It seems that the action just happens on its own in a spontaneous and natural way. We could call this transpersonal agency or, alternatively, nonagency. I don't think it matters. There is a sense of empowerment and efficacy that does not refer to anyone, or at least not to our familiar sense of being a separate self. There is a sense of something coming through us, as if we are a vessel for its expression. Further, we are not attached to the result of the action. The action is complete in itself. We act and let go.

When we are free of fear and shame, unconcerned about how we look or sound to others, and attuned to the need of the moment, life moves freely through us. This power is inherently benevolent and live-giving. Some Buddhists take a bodhisattva vow to dedicate their life to the well-being of others. This is a beautiful intention. When we are released, even temporarily, from the illusion of being a separate self, this intention is spontaneously actualized. We don't have to *try* to be a servant of the whole; we are one.

"Unwinding Gut Terror"

When I work with people, our investigation tends to spontaneously focus most often on three areas of the body: the heart area at mid-chest, the solar plexus, and the base of the spine. Other areas such as the head, throat, and lower belly do arise and need attention depending upon our conditioning; however, they tend to be secondary. While the whole body is important, the heart area, solar plexus, and base of the spine tend to hold the deepest contractions that veil the recognition and embodiment of our true nature. They also tend to interact, so a shift in one center affects another.

In the following experiential conversation, we'll see these phenomena, particularly the intimate connection between the knot in the gut and an underlying feeling of terror. Sam shares his experience of terror and shakiness that was stirred up by listening to my online talk about the ground. At first he describes a strong burning sensation in the solar plexus, followed by a sudden unwinding of tension as if an inner rope has released. This release allows his attention to descend (slide down) and settle into a sense of being deeply grounded.

Sam: [That talk] really shook some stuff loose. It's very juicy over here right now. My heart is pounding. There's this burning in the solar plexus. I'm even shaking. I'm not even sure what the question is anymore. There's something big going on here. Talk of the ground has turned it all on.

John: Good, let's sit with it together, okay? I invite you to attend to your experience, and I'll be with you. Take time to be quiet and attune with what's happening, what you're sensing and feeling. [*Pause*] Feel free to share whenever you are moved to.

Sam: So the energy is . . . the terror is subsiding, and it is shifting down lower in the belly. It has a different tone, and it's not echoing up here [*touches throat*] as much.

John: So attention is dropping down. There's probably more safety.

Sam: Hmm. Yeah, yeah. [*Pause*] There's more weight to it now. Like something is being drawn down.

John: Just allow that to happen. No effort. Just an inner, *Okay, yes.*

Sam: It's like sliding slowly down a slide. There's still a little bit of . . . echoes around the solar plexus, belly area.

John: Probably some concern. Is it safe to let go?

Sam: Yeah. [*Pause*] It is quieter. There's a scariness, but it's not scary-scary. Okay-scary?

John: Tolerable scary. Maybe exciting?

Sam: Oh, *exciting* might be a better word for that! [*Pause*] There's more resting now. The word you used isn't quite coming . . .

John: Settling?

Sam: *Settling* is a great word for it. Something that was very wound up has been able to relax.

John: The description "to unwind" is common. Melting, unwinding, settling.

Sam: As if there was a rope wound around something, and it just flopped out. Hmm. [*Pause*] I was going to ask you how to fix my throat, but this is just fine the way it is.

John: It takes care of itself, doesn't it?

Sam: It does.

John: Your image of the rope unwinding is also quite apt because the rope is how we try to hold ourself up and in. And then we realize we don't need to.

Sam: Yeah. It's hard to imagine moving from such an uncomfortable place to such a comfortable resting state.

John: Interesting, isn't it?

Sam: Yeah. That was very uncomfortable a moment ago.

John: We lean into our experience with curiosity, affection, vulnerability, and honesty, and it becomes a portal.

Sam: Yeah.

John: Discomfort is actually a pathway as we explore together.

Sam: Thank you. That is something I would have run from on my own, I think.

John: This is a good point. We have to discover that it is safe to go here, and often we feel unsafe to deal with it by ourself. It can be helpful to have someone else there who is not afraid. It could be a friend or a helper of some kind. We may only need help a few times. Or if it is rockier, we may need more regular support to discover we have the resources, the resilience, the capacity to be with this on our own. That brings a sense of greater autonomy and self-trust.

Sam: Thank you so much, John.

John: It's a beautiful sharing. I appreciate it, too.

Two important insights arose from this exchange. First, that our fear can be a portal to our depths; and second, sometimes we need someone else to be there with us as we turn toward what we have spent our lives running from. Even though we did not uncover the source of Sam's terror in this brief exchange, it quickly resolved itself, at least temporarily. My guess is that, early on, Sam learned to "rope himself in" as a way to feel safe, an unconscious attempt to hold himself that also bound and strangled his aliveness. This became clear as his fear quickly transformed into excitement and gratitude. It is likely that he will need to traverse this territory several more times in order to stabilize this sense of being deeply settled.

Safety was a crucial factor in this meeting. Even though Sam was in a highly activated and vulnerable state characterized by terror and a visceral shaking, he also realized "something juicy" was happening. He trusted me and himself enough to come forward in front of a large online group and openly explore his experience. He felt safe enough to let go of the illusion of being in control.

Meditation
Releasing the Illusion of Control

Find a place where you won't be disturbed for a few minutes, and sit comfortably upright, if possible. Close your eyes and take several deep, slow breaths. (*Pause*)

Let your attention drop down and into the core of your body. (*Pause*)

Now bring your attention to your solar plexus. (*Pause*)

Imagine you can breathe directly into and out of the solar plexus. (*Pause*)

Feel into the space behind your solar plexus and your whole body. (*Pause*)

Relax back into this background space. (*Pause*)

Be willing to let go of any attempt to control your experience and let it be completely just as it is. (*Long pause*)

Notice if there is a separate self that is controlling your experience. If so, be curious and ask yourself, *Who or what is in control?* This is another form of self-inquiry. Notice what happens. (*Long pause*)

Stay with this exploration for as long as you'd like. You can also practice releasing the illusion of control when you are active during the day.

9

Survival Fear I

I've lived through some terrible things in my
life, some of which actually happened.

—(widely attributed to) Mark Twain

I think it's fair to say that most of us have been terrified at some time in our lives—not just afraid but *terrified*—that we would die. I had a brief brush with this terror as I was starting to ford Mono Creek in the High Sierras in 2017. The creek, swollen by snowmelt, was two to three feet deep in the middle and perhaps twenty feet across. There was no guideline to hold on to, and amid the swift current and large smooth stones I could not find the creek bed with my trekking poles. With one false step I could lose my balance and be swept downstream, losing my unbuckled backpack and possibly my life if my head hit a boulder. Although my backpacking partner Ken had just made it safely across, I hesitated for almost a minute, thigh-deep in the near-freezing water, feeling shaky in my legs. And then I stepped back. My inner knowing was not giving me a green light to cross. A few minutes later I found a log further upstream and easily crossed.

In this case, I was facing real physical danger. However, as adults, we often experience irrational survival fears that originate in child-hood. The author and spiritual teacher Byron Katie has noted that reality is almost always kinder than our thoughts. Most of the terrible things we fear don't end up happening. Yet every once in a while, they do. This kind of terror, whether induced by real or imagined events, leaves a deep imprint in our psyches and nervous systems.

Clearing the Basement

When I explore this level of terror with people, I think of it as "clear-ing the basement." As our system opens up, this buried material inevitably gets flushed out. If the psyche is like a house, we spend most of our waking state on the ground floor dealing with ordinary events and relationships. Unless there is a crisis—an inner or outer earthquake—we rarely visit the basement. Yet it is the basement where we store our most difficult, life-altering experiences, locking them away in dark, compressed storage rooms. If we are sincerely interested in embodying our true nature, we will need to allow these rooms to unlock themselves. If we are willing, the light of awareness will eventually infuse and liberate these dark spaces. When this hap-pens, it is as if windows and doors suddenly appear in the basement, flooding it with light and air. Rusty locks and closed doors pop open on their own, freeing trapped vital energies and essential qualities of being, such as innocence and playfulness, to join the whole system.

Often as one level of the basement clears, another reveals itself. I've found that there are subbasements and sub-subbasements that hold ever more primal levels of fear, dread, shame, and aloneness. I've also found the deeper the descent, the more collective and archetypal the experience becomes. We'll talk more about some of the deepest underground dimensions in chapter 12, with Carl Jung as our guide. Beyond this is the groundless ground of open awareness.

Facing the Dark Abyss

Survival fear localizes at the base of the spine as a subtle somatic contraction. Some people experience it as a more generalized tension in the pelvic bowl. For others it seems to localize at the perineum. The exact location isn't important. It is the same palpable clench *down there*. Under real or apparent threat, our body-mind instinctively withdraws and inwardly freezes in order to be safe. When this contraction becomes chronic, we mis-take it as our ground.

For most of us there is a large gulf between this false ground of contraction and the true ground of spacious openness. To the ordinary mind, this gulf appears as a dark abyss. For some, there is an invitation to jump. For others, to fall. Most of us instinctively hold back. There was a period in my life when I had a recurring dream of speeding in a car along a serpentine mountain road, losing control, and plunging off a steep cliff to my imminent death. Yet I never died in these dreams. Rather, I experienced a joyful dissolution and freedom. While at first I was terrified to lose control and fly off a cliff, in time I came to enjoy it. My dreams were signaling the conscious emergence of my true ground. What appeared in these dreams as physical death was in fact an opening to a deeper reality. The abyss is not what it seems.

There are two distinct yet closely related levels of conditioning that contribute to this contraction at the base of the spine: psychological and existential. By psychological, I mean the specific conditioning that we experience growing up in our family of origin. By existential, I mean the general challenges of life that we all must face regardless of our individual conditioning. In this chapter I review the most common psychological causes of our survival fear: abandonment, engulfment, attack, and falling apart. Sometimes they happen all at once.

Fear of Abandonment

After decades of guiding inner work with clients and students, I have found that the most common survival fear is abandonment. To be left on one's own as an infant or young child is terrifying because we cannot take care of ourself. We are completely dependent on our caretakers for physical protection and nurturance as well as emotional connection. We need to sense and feel on multiple levels that we are connected. Our life literally depends on it.

The fear of abandonment has many forms, including the fear of being alone, being disconnected, not belonging, being rejected, being left behind, and separation. Have you ever experienced any of these, particularly in their raw emotional and somatic form? We experience a form of this as adults when we go through a wrenching emotional breakup with a lover, friend, or family member. Take a moment here to reflect on your experience and how tender it is to brush against it. For this reason, we tend to completely avoid feeling this fear. No wonder! It can feel overwhelming and unbearable.

As a result, we often unconsciously organize our lives around trying to avoid feeling abandoned by numbing, distracting, or distancing ourselves from it. We inwardly split ourself, drug ourself, drive ourself, and even try to meditate and transcend ourself. Above all, we don't depend on anyone else or let them get too close. In other words, we abandon ourself in order not to feel abandoned. We are then quick to abandon others before they abandon us. We do so in degrees, first by distancing from our inner experience and then by distancing from others.

This self-abandonment brings its own special grief. Certainly we grieve many kinds of losses—loved ones, places, precious objects, identities, and even belief systems. But our deepest grief happens when we abandon ourself. This nameless grief is particularly hard to identify because it does not refer to someone or something. In fact, we have lost touch with our true home, our wholeness, our essential self. To regain and sustain an inner sense of homecoming, we must consciously navigate our fear of abandonment and its related grief.

Fear and grief can be primary portals to our being; however, we need to be well-resourced in order to adequately open to and integrate this material. The more we are able to contact some degree of presence in the form of spacious, loving awareness, the more we can genuinely welcome our abandoned self without an agenda to change it. As we've seen, this innocent welcoming is crucial.

Interestingly, a two-way trust often needs to be established between our adult self and our abandoned-child self. The adult does not trust that the child will not act out in harmful ways if it is given space to feel and be as it is. And the child does not trust that it is really wanted and that it won't be rejected again. When the experience of being abandoned is particularly acute due to early traumatic ruptures or poor bonding, our inner child experiences a preverbal hell realm of terror, despair, and aloneness. Reconnection happens more through sensing, feeling, and gentle physical touch than through words or thoughts. It takes time for this mutual trust to unfold. And since the initial rupture was relational, the healing almost always happens within an attuned relationship.

As children, we need to feel warmly and securely held, to be lovingly embraced. Abandoned children do not feel this. Instead, they learn to hold themselves tightly—too tightly. When I offer a guided meditation, I often encourage people to feel the weight of their body being held by gravity and to relax into the sense of being held. Listeners who have not experienced being held as children often have difficulty with this step. At first it is foreign to them. It takes them more time to access the sense of being held by something greater, even if it is gravity. When they do, something that has been tightly wound in their core begins to release.

When we've felt abandoned or badly neglected, we conclude that we are not worth caring for. This makes it difficult to invest in our own self-care as well as our own life. If our core needs for safety, connection, mirroring, and holding are not recognized and met, we conclude that we are unimportant or burdensome to others. As a result, we find ourself constantly devaluing our basic needs and apologizing for ourself. Sometimes we even believe that we don't deserve to exist or that our life doesn't matter. This is a devastating belief. I recall being shocked when I first encountered it in my therapeutic work. Have you ever believed and felt this way about yourself?

The other day I uncovered this belief while working with one of my students. She was disturbed that she was still falling into old habits of not caring for herself despite having had many clear experiences of her true nature as open awareness. Why was it that she couldn't align her actions with her inner knowing? As she dropped her self-judgments and innocently inquired into her experience, she encountered the belief that her life didn't matter and realized that part of her wanted to stay hidden and small. It felt safer to self-medicate with alcohol and food than to open. She then saw an image of a small frozen corpse. She realized that her infant self needed to feel safely held before she would venture out and explore the world. She then spontaneously imagined embracing her little girl in the midst of a circle of loving friends. As she did so, the sense of being inwardly frozen began to thaw.

Sadly, some students of the no-self teachings in Eastern contemplative traditions confuse this sense of not existing or not mattering with the emptiness of self that is described as the fruition of the spiritual search. Feeling a profound sense of lack or deficiency is *not* what these wisdom teachings are pointing to. Hameed Ali (pen name: A. H. Almaas), the founder of the Diamond Approach, makes a very useful distinction between deficient and full emptiness.[1] The self that does not feel it deserves to exist is a deflated or deficient version of the separate self. It feels alone, cut off, and disconnected from the whole of life. True emptiness, on the other hand, refers to the sense of being open to, and not separate from, the whole of life. In the latter case, we are empty of our self-constructed identity as a separate self.

If we carefully inquire into the beliefs that we don't deserve to exist or don't matter, they fall away on their own. There is no question of deserving or not deserving, mattering or not mattering. These are mental constructs. Who we are can never be bound by any construct, negative or positive. The medicine for self-abandonment is multilevel self-intimacy. This means we are willing to feel and sense what is here in our body right now. It also means we question our core limiting beliefs from our deepest knowing. Finally, it means we rest in and as awareness.

A Prescription for Self-Intimacy

Feel your feelings.
Sense your sensations.
Question your core limiting beliefs.
Rest in and as awareness.

If we do not feel our feelings, sense our sensations, or question our core limiting beliefs from our deepest knowing, we will project them onto others. And, not surprisingly, we will also project them onto the unknown. Specifically, if we have not resolved our abandonment issues, we will not feel safe to let go of our illusion of control and open ourselves to life. Somewhere deep in our psyche, life will appear as an abandoning mother or father, and spacious awareness will seem like a cold, abandoning abyss. Why would anyone want to open to that? There is a visceral resistance to doing so. If we are interested in truly embodying awareness, sooner or later we must face and resolve our fear of abandonment. This requires the clarity of understanding, the courage to feel what has been suppressed, and the willingness to open to the Unknown.

"No One Is Coming"

In the following conversation during an online event, Amanda first experiences a lovely opening of space down and behind her body. She then encounters resistance related to the core belief that "no one is coming" and comes face to face with an underlying despair of separation. Beneath this, she can sense a deeper ground, a space of truth and light. When she allows her despair to be held in awareness, there is a release. This is an interesting variation on the theme of abandonment where despair, rather than fear, is the predominant experience. The two—terror and despair—often go together.

Amanda: There's a [release] down and behind that's working together. [*Pause*] [*Chuckles*] So I'm just feeling my way into the avoidance. Some time ago you had us think about a core limiting belief. Mine was something along the lines of "No one's coming." It was definitely an abandonment-separation. It feels like the core-core separation. It's almost like there's a fascia. I can feel the separation, and it's all the way up and down my spine. And just behind, beneath, and below that . . . is the home where separation simply does not exist.

John: Our home ground.

Amanda: Yeah. So, I'm eternally grateful I can feel that.

John: Absolutely.

Amanda: I'm wondering if there might be some advice [from] you other than when I notice the avoidance to stop and ask myself if that's what I really want.

John: It is good to notice avoidance and then stop and open to it. Right now, because you are very attuned with this home ground, this openness, and you are also aware of some subtle resistance, simply welcome that resistance.

Amanda: [*Sighs*]

John: Just allow it and notice what happens.

Amanda: I can feel the familiar constriction around my spine, the top and the bottom. [*Pause*] Oh, there's just despair. Almost more despair than fear. [*Voice trembles.*]

John: That makes sense.

Amanda: [*tears*] And the despair is that "I am alone and none of this beauty is possible. It is just made up or something."

John: The despair of separation.

Amanda: Yeah, exactly.

John: Just allow this despair.

Amanda: [*chuckles*] Allow it? Yechh!

John: This home ground of awareness does not resist it. The mind does.

Amanda: [*sighs*] Oh. [*Pause*] I feel like I'm in a *Star Trek* show and it's like I'm trying to land where people come from one place to the next, you know. And it's [*making a sound expressing difficulty and then chuckling*] because I can feel when you just said . . . this despair is just held.

John: It is, indeed.

Amanda: There's no question.

John: This is where pinpointing is helpful. To name the despair of separation and to recognize that it is held. And then be with that. Okay?

Amanda: Yes, thank you.

In this exploration, Amanda encountered the "core-core" sense of separation that ran like fascia—stringy connective tissue—up and down her spine. Beneath and behind this she gratefully sensed a home where there was no separation. We can guess that this belief and visceral core contraction started very early in her life when she felt desperately alone and separate, when no one came for her. There was a deep despair that she did not want to feel—yechh! Yet with a little guidance and support, she was able to allow it. She then felt as if her body was being teleported like a *Star Trek* crew member.

This is a rich tactile metaphor because as these core holding patterns release, it can feel as if our body is being remade. Our body feels less like something solid and more like a vibrant energy field. Where are we being teleported? To right here! Rather than being "beamed up," we are being "beamed down" into this moment.

Fears of Engulfment, Attack, and Falling Apart

In addition to fearing abandonment, people often experience the fear of being engulfed, attacked, or falling apart. These are all distinct forms of feeling annihilated. It's been very interesting to see how important it is for my students and former clients to accurately name what they are terrified of. Before they do, their acute fear remains vague. They know that they feel ill at ease, agitated, hypervigilant, and unable to deeply rest. However, once they can accurately name their fear and gauge that it is in fact the terror of annihilation, it starts to take form. It becomes an object in awareness, something that is in them but that does not fully define or overshadow who they are. Their terror becomes approachable.

The fear of engulfment is the fear of being swallowed by another. Have you ever been in a group where one member completely dominates the space, sucking up all the oxygen in the room? They feel compelled to constantly display their superiority due to a sense of entitlement as well as underlying insecurity and sense of lack. This narcissistic behavior happens most commonly with men. Now imagine growing up with a father like this. Perhaps you have!

The polarity of this is where a parent is so collapsed and needy that they are unavailable to really listen to or be with their children. Instead, they overtly or covertly pull on their children's attention and energy in order to be rescued from their own suffering. Their depression and fear feels like a dark hole. This form is more common with women who have been severely dominated and devalued throughout their life. Parents with bipolar disorder can easily engulf their children with both their manic and depressive mood swings.

If we grow up in a family where one of our parents is like this, it can feel as if we are being erased, swallowed, or smothered. Our own needs, feelings, and authentic expression become completely subservient to our parent. It is as if we can't breathe; we are without boundaries and cannot exist as we are. It is a terrifying experience. In this situation, healing comes by gradually recognizing and validating our core needs and feelings, being able to set appropriate boundaries, and authentically expressing our unique way of being. We must also undo the burdensome belief that we are here to rescue or fulfill our parents, which is an impossible task. We are neither their saviors nor their trophies; nor are our children these for us.

The fear of being attacked also induces the fear of annihilation. If we have been brought up in a home where a parent—usually the father—explodes with rage and lashes out verbally or physically at us, we learn to hide, be as small as possible, or become invisible. We also internalize the attacks and believe that we deserve them. It feels profoundly unsafe to be home, and as a result, we dissociate. If these attacks happen over a long period of time, they often induce a complex post-traumatic stress disorder that takes dedicated time and attention to unwind.

The fear of falling apart or fragmenting can also feel annihilating. When this happens, it feels like our center will not hold and we will irrevocably shatter. People who've experienced a brief reactive psychosis due to unbearable emotional stress experience this. To regulate their nervous system, they need to be calmed and feel contained.

Ancestral and Collective Streams

We also carry the terror of our ancestors. This toxic heirloom is passed down from generation to generation. If our recent ancestors have been terrorized, the impact is greater. I have a friend whose Jewish parents were in their twenties when they were forced to live in basements and cellars during four years of Nazi occupation in the Netherlands. Every few months they had to move to another hiding place in order to stay safe. When the war ended, they discovered that most of their remaining family had perished in the death camps. They were never able to talk about their experiences and feelings with their daughters, who, as a result, unconsciously carried this trauma for many years.

At a recent retreat, a Jewish man shared that he both longed for and was terrified to fully open the depths of his heart out of fear that it would "be crushed under a Nazi jackboot." A day later he spontaneously comforted a German woman who was racked with shame and a feeling of profound cultural groundlessness given how her grandfather's generation had acted before and during World War II. I was deeply moved to see her resting her head on his shoulder after she had shared her feelings of not belonging anywhere. It was a quiet, poignant gesture of healing arising nearly eighty years after a war that had traumatized their grandparents' generation.

Ancestral trauma also follows along racial and gender lines. The United States has a dark stain of racism toward enslaved Africans, its Indigenous peoples, and any immigrants labeled as "other" that Americans continue to uncomfortably grapple with. Echoes of this traumatic history reverberate in people's psyches, whether they are oppressed or oppressors. With gender-related trauma, I've worked in depth with a number of women who have uncovered a profound fear of being persecuted and killed if they fully stepped into their wisdom and power. For many centuries, wise and powerful women were demonized, terrorized, and burned at the stake as witches. This searing image surfaces from the collective unconscious in many women as they move to take their rightful seat as fully empowered members and leaders of society.

Being with the Fear of Annihilation

Most people are unable to navigate the fear of annihilation on their own, for good reason. It is simply too overwhelming to deal with, especially at first. We need to be well resourced to be fully with it. If we are not, there is a real risk of being pulled back into it and becoming retraumatized. It really helps to have someone with us who has faced and, to some extent, navigated this terrain themselves. We need the warm support and clear guidance of another human being who is unafraid of the dark. This may be a seasoned therapist, counselor, coach, or spiritual guide. It may also be a mature friend, lover, or family member who has some psychological understanding and ability to attune as the psyche begins to spontaneously unwind itself. Don't be afraid or ashamed to ask for help. We all need it with this material.

Internally, our most important resource is presence—spacious, wakeful awareness. Once we have been able to recognize the fear of annihilation by locating it somatically as a clench in the belly and/or pelvic bowl, and once we've found some form of its associated belief that *I'm going to die*, we can let it go and turn our attention to *this*, which is always aware.

Take a few minutes to rest back into open, spacious awareness. Once you have a sense of this openness, welcome the terror with curiosity and affection. Let it come to you; don't go into it. Simply notice what happens without an agenda to fix or change anything. If your experience becomes too intense, open your eyes, look around at your current surroundings, and remind yourself where you are and that you are safe. Once you feel calmer, continue your exploration again until there's a natural inclination to stop. If any shifts, releases, or insights arise, let them in. Let your system update from the past to the present moment. Usually this process of release happens over time in layers and requires rinsing and repeating multiple times.

Meditation
Welcoming Terror

Find a quiet place where you won't be disturbed and, if possible, sit comfortably upright with your feet on the floor. Close your eyes and take several slow, deep breaths. (*Pause*)

Remind yourself that there is nowhere to go, nothing to get, and no problem to solve. Then allow your attention to drop down and into the trunk of your body. (*Pause*)

Sense the center of your chest and imagine that you can breathe directly into and out of this center. As you do so, evoke a feeling of kindness for yourself and let it in. (*Pause*)

Now sense your lower belly and imagine that you can breathe directly into and out of this center. As you do so, evoke a feeling of safety and let it in. (*Pause*)

If the fear of annihilation arises, be open to experiencing it, but don't search for or evoke it. Simply be willing to experience it if it is there. Notice any contraction in your body and feelings of fear. If nothing arises, simply rest in meditation and ignore the following prompts. (*Pause*)

After a few minutes of feeling and sensing, be open to discovering the specific belief that accompanies this acute fear. Keep it simple and short, and check inwardly to see if you have stated it as clearly as possible. There will be a sense of "rightness" when you have. (*Pause*)

When you're clear on the belief, let it go, along with the associated sensations and feelings. Shift your attention to a sense of open, spacious awareness, first behind and then all around you. Attune with this awareness so it becomes palpable. Rest in this space for several minutes. (*Long pause*)

When you feel ready, welcome the terror of annihilation into this sense of spacious awareness. Don't go retrieve it. Let it come into you. (*Pause*)

Don't try to make anything happen. Simply note what happens. (*Pause*)

What happens in your body-mind when contraction and confusion are met by openness? Don't force any reactions. Just notice. (*Pause*)

If there are any shifts, releases, or spontaneous insights, let them in. (*Long pause*)

When you feel this meditation coming to a natural close, open your eyes and take a minute or two to reorient yourself before engaging in other activity. If possible, spend some time outside.

10

Survival Fear II

The most important thing is to find out the most important thing.

—Shunryu Suzuki Roshi, lecture, 1967

Regardless of our childhood and ancestral conditioning, we all face the same existential questions and challenges. The truth is, we have a brief time on earth to live as fully as we can—five or six hundred million breaths if we are lucky—before we step off stage. What is the most important thing while we are here? What do we devote our attention and energy to? I invite you to reflect upon the following values and consider which are the most important for you.

- Experiencing safety, comfort, and pleasure
- Being seen and valued by others

- Leaving a legacy
- Helping others
- Making a better world
- Loving and being loved
- Being authentic
- Discovering your true nature

There is no right or wrong response to this values inventory, as our values often change with time and life experience. Regardless of what you chose, we often need to address basic survival and social needs before we are ready to investigate our essential nature. When this shift is given the space to happen, love and wisdom become increasingly important. We start to question our unconscious grip of separation. Our view and experience of life starts to open up. We may discover that life and death are not what we think.

On a clear November morning, I sat in meditation with a friend as he was dying. We were in his newly constructed home overlooking Mount Tamalpais, north of San Francisco. Rob was an organizer, a builder, and a longtime student of the dharma and nondual teachings. Gregarious, good-humored, and gracious with his friends, he never took himself very seriously. After a three-year bout with lung cancer, his health took a sudden downturn. Despite being cared for by hospice, he experienced excruciating pain in the mornings. After careful reflection, he decided to end his life by having a hospice physician help him self-administer a fatal cocktail. He invited a small group of friends and his sister to be with him.

As we gathered in a circle around his bed, Rob expressed his gratitude and appreciation for us, as we did for him. I read Rumi's "On the Day I Die," shared Jean Klein's advice "to die with the dying person," and invited everyone to let go and be open as we sat with him. Before taking the medication, he made a small bow and said, "Please, be happy." Rob slipped into a coma after five minutes and his slow, quiet breathing continued for another forty minutes or so before ending. I sat peacefully nearby with closed eyes, expecting nothing. After about a half hour, I sensed an increasingly strong ascending light and felt a quiet ecstasy, as if a veil was parting and a luminous overhead dimension was opening.

Later, as I left the house and stepped outside, my visual field was unusually clear. The world seemed illumined. Certainly Rob's body had died, but what was this flood of upwelling light? I had witnessed a great mystery, a poignant and sacred transition. I had also received Rob's final gift: a foretaste of my own passing.

When we investigate the ground level of our identity, it can feel as if we are coming face to face with our own death. Our deepest existential fears and doubts arise. Typically they constellate around the following questions:

- Is it safe to completely let go?
- If I do, what happens to my connection with others? Will I be all alone?
- Am I limited to this body?
- Can I trust myself and life?

Let's explore each of these questions individually. I invite you to sense which ones may be particularly resonate for you.

Safety

Sometimes when I work with people who are deeply engaged in the process of letting go, they feel their old identity falling away and wonder if they are going to die. I reassure them that the only thing that will die is an old self-image and story, that nothing essential dies. We fear that if we see through who we have taken our self to be, our body will die; we mistakenly conflate our self-image with our body. It is true that a kind of death happens, but it is not the body's. Rather, it is the end of who we thought we were, along with all of the feelings and sensations that go with it.

As long as we see ourselves as separate from the whole, we feel unsafe. As individual beings, we are like waves; as Being, we are like a boundless ocean. We are both the wave and the ocean; formed and formless. When we take ourself only as a wave and forget our oceanic nature, we live in psychological fear. But when we remember our oceanic nature, the fear of losing ourself falls away and biological fear continues to a lesser degree. For example, the startle reflex remains and we continue to protect and care for our body, but the idea of our eventual physical death is no longer a threat.

People also ask if they will lose their sanity during this process. I assure them that the opposite is true; they will gain it. In fact, it is a kind of insanity to view ourselves as being separate from the whole of life. It is true that we are each unique, and it is important that we individuate, find our own truth, and live in accord with it. This will look different for each of us. But individuating does not mean becoming more separate. It means uncovering and orienting to our inherent wholeness. As we discover our shared ground, we are freer to be just as we are.

It can be disorienting to let go of who we think we are. It is like discovering that we are not the character in a play that we have been taking ourself to be: *What do you mean I am not Hamlet, Prince of Denmark?* Of course most of us don't pretend to be princes or princesses, but we have our own modest and equally compelling version of identity. It can be unnerving to discover that while I may be playing a particular role and be seen this way by others, it's not who I really am. As our mask of identity starts to slip, a different reality unfolds. We become less of a known quantity and more of a living mystery. No box can confine us.

Disorientation usually precedes reorientation. Once we've dropped our old suit of clothes, it can take a while to acclimate to being dressed so simply. We are accustomed to having an image to project and protect, so it's normal to feel simultaneously disarmed and freed as this old habit falls away.

Inquiry
Inquiry into Safety

Find a place where you won't be disturbed. If possible, sit comfortably upright with your feet on the ground. Close your eyes and take several slow, deep breaths. (*Pause*)

Remind yourself that there is no problem to solve, nowhere to go, and nothing to get. Allow your attention to drop down and into the core of your body. (*Pause*)

Once you feel settled in, ask yourself, *Who wants to be safe?* Then let the question go and be quietly receptive. (*Pause*)

If the response is *I do* or *Me*, ask again, *Who is this I or me that wants to be safe?* (*Pause*)

Continue to quietly sit with this question for another five to ten minutes. Be sure to let in any spontaneous insights, feelings, and sensations that arise. Return to this question whenever you feel unsafe. As with other inquiries, if nothing arises during your investigation, feel free to modify the question or completely let it go. It may not be relevant for you.

Connection and Aloneness

As we embark on this descent, we often fear losing connection with those we love. We may wonder, *Who will follow me as I let go? Will I be all alone?* There is some truth to this fear. As we are shedding or completely dropping our fictitious identity as a separate self, relationships will change. We will be less interested in forms of contact that are designed to reassure the "little me." Throughout this journey, authenticity becomes paramount. As a result, inauthentic relationships are challenged. If they can't up-level, they tend to diminish or fall away. It is likely that we will lose some old friends. The good news is our authentic relationships deepen, and in time, we find kindred spirits.

Connection is a subtle theme. Relatively speaking, we connect with one another (or not) on myriad levels: physically, emotionally, mentally, and energetically. When we connect well, there is an exchange of energy and information that we find pleasurable and enlivening. Yet when we meet on the essential level of being, our normal concept of connection or relationship no longer fits. On this level, being meets itself as the apparent other. Strange as it may sound, this most intimate of meetings is the least personal. Thich Nhat Hanh, the renowned Vietnamese Buddhist teacher, called this *interbeing*, a felicitous term.[1] If you've ever relaxed into an innocent gazing practice with a friend or partner, you've probably experienced this surprising quality of nonpersonal intimacy.[2]

It is quite normal to fear being alone as we let go of our conventional identity. We are very conditioned to depend upon others for reassurance that we exist and have value. We rely on this mirroring to help keep our self-image intact. As we begin to deeply question our conventional identity, we may find that fewer people will be able to relate to our experience. This brings up the fear of aloneness. However, in this place of spacious awareness, we discover that aloneness is not what we imagined. Instead of entering into isolation, we come out of it. It becomes clearer that our apparent aloneness is a portal to a profound impersonal intimacy with life. As we deepen in our exploration, we discover a growing sense of autonomy and confidence. Yet even as we are able to stand more on our own, increasingly free of others' approval or disapproval, we also open to our interdependence with everyone and everything. This is very different from the posture of the well-defended separate self that asserts a false independence. Once we're in touch with our deepest ground, we don't need to assert our autonomy; we discover it.

Inquiry

Inquiry into Connection

Find a place where you won't be disturbed. If possible, sit comfortably upright with your feet on the ground. Close your eyes and take several slow, deep breaths. (*Pause*)

Remind yourself that there is no problem to solve, nowhere to go, and nothing to get. Allow your attention to drop down and into the core of your body. (*Pause*)

Once you're settled in, ask yourself, *What happens to my sense of connection with others when I let go of who I take myself to be?*

Continue sitting with this question as long as it feels fruitful. Let in any insights and shifts that may arise.

Body Identification

Our attachment to and identification with our body runs extraordinarily deep—deeper than our attachment to our beliefs and feelings. The sense that "I am this body" is primal, deeply instinctual, and largely unconscious. "I am *in* this body" and "This body *belongs* to me" are corollary identities. These are such deeply rooted convictions that we rarely question them. But we would do well to. In fact, if we want to fully embody our understanding, we must question and see through this deepest of identifications.

This root identification lies deep underground in the psyche. It is a powerful energetic knot in the sub-subbasement. This is where consciousness identifies itself with form. Over the years I've had a handful of clients and students report remembering the moment when they entered their mother's womb and identified with their body. They describe this event as a profound contraction, an entrance into a much denser plane of existence. While I cannot assess the validity of these claims, I am impressed by their similarity.

It almost always takes time to unwind this primal knot of identification because we are so used to localizing ourself as this body; it is such a deeply familiar contraction. But I want to be clear here that questioning and releasing this knot is not a dissociative escape. It is not done out of avoidance or aversion. Instead, it comes out of the initial intuition and then experiential discovery that "I am not *just* this body." We realize that we are this body *and* we are so much more, infinitely so. We do not bypass, deny, or refuse our body. Rather, we embrace it as a sacred *expression* of consciousness. Once we discover the context of spacious awareness or presence, the body is free to unfold within us. Our body is also not what we think it is; its true nature is spacious and vibrant.

Inquiry
Inquiry into Body Identification

Find a place where you won't be disturbed. If possible, sit comfortably upright with your feet on the ground. Close your eyes and take several slow, deep breaths. (*Pause*)

Remind yourself that there is no problem to solve, nowhere to go, and nothing to get. Allow your attention to drop down and into the core of your body. (*Pause*)

When you're settled, ask yourself, *Am I just this body?* and let go of the question. (*Pause*)

Continue sitting with this question as long as it feels fruitful. Let in any insights and shifts as they arise.

Basic Trust

Our mistrust of life also resides somatically as a contraction at the base of the spine. When there is a basic mistrust, we feel a clench. As basic trust unfolds, this clench releases. Trust in ourself and in life are the same thing. It is not an egoic trust in our individual capacity;

we know we have limits as an individual. Nor is it a trust that everything will work out as we wish; we know our plans will sometimes be thwarted and we will encounter difficult circumstances. We are not exempt from accidents, illness, and disabilities. This is not a child's naïve trust; it is an open-eyed trust that accepts that things happen as they need to. It is a full embrace that includes the most difficult aspect of human life: our intentional cruelty to one another. It is an unconditional trust in life, no matter what.

The mind is incapable of such an embrace, no matter how spiritually educated it may be. Instead, this embrace is a spontaneous gesture of our true nature. Spacious loving awareness, not the conditioned mind, embraces what is. This is not a passive acceptance. Part of "what is" includes our creative response to suffering, how we are moved to address it. We see things as they are and then respond. This is a movement of love and wisdom.

Inquiry
Inquiry into Trust

Find a place where you won't be disturbed. If possible, sit comfortably upright with your feet on the ground. Close your eyes and take several slow, deep breaths. (*Pause*)

Remind yourself that there is no problem to solve, nowhere to go, and nothing to get. Allow your attention to drop down and into the core of your body. (*Pause*)

Once you're settled, ask yourself, *Is there something in me that trusts life as it is?* (*Pause*)

Continue sitting with this question as long as it feels fruitful. Let in any insights and shifts as they arise.

"I'm Being Swept Away by Life"

In the following exchange during an online course, Carol describes experiencing calmness, then a sense of dissolution and nausea, and finally a vibrant silence. She discovers that, despite her dissolution, she is still here. While we dialogue, she experiences a powerful downpouring energy. As she trusts her inner knowing, she opens to two fears: being swallowed by the ground and being swept away by the river of life.

Carol: When you opened our meeting today in silence and we met each other, all I could feel was fear. Then in the meditation I felt a dissolution and it nauseated me. I went through several rounds of survival response. I just stayed, orienting to your voice and coming to safety again. [There were] several rounds of this felt-sense of calm, which for me is dissolution.

My conditioning is that I am being swallowed by the ground. After going through several rounds of trying to protect and control my body, I finally allowed [myself] to speak, "Here I am. Nothing happened to me." Then there was a vibrant silence—so calm, so peaceful. I can feel it while my body is still trembling and vibrating. Can I just breathe with that? [*Pause*] I hold on by discounting myself. That's painful to notice. Can I know that I know? [*Tears*]

John: You do know . . . stay with this true seeing.

Carol: [*tears*] There's a streaming right now. Going down into my legs and then out.

John: A downpouring. There's a knowing, let it in.

Carol: [*tears*] So, it feels like my body is the container. Can my container grow? Can it hold more of what is coming in without deflecting?

John: Without deflecting, just allowing. It's a process. The body adjusts to the influx of the light of awareness.

Carol: Yeah, because for me that aliveness has felt threatening.

John: There's a fear of aliveness.

Carol: I feel so much right now. It's amping up its volume, especially in my legs.

John: There's a downpouring and the root chakra is opening. You can sense that because there's a streaming of energy down into the legs and feet. So the energy body is opening up. It's very natural. Just breathe, trust. This is a natural opening and acclimation process.

Carol: The reaction of my body is again fear. As I feel this, there's a closing in my stomach again producing nausea.

John: There's a fear of losing control, I imagine. There's something very important here. We fear death and annihilation, but we also fear life.

Carol: Yes.

John: Because they are both unknown. And, in truth, they are not separate.

Carol: Yeah. The storyline is that I'm being swept away by life, and I have nothing to hold on to. This is the river of life. There's nothing to hold on to.

John: It's liberating to realize that there's nothing we need to hold on to. This opening is completely trustworthy. I'll leave you with this.

Carol: Yes. It feels like a good end point.

John: Give yourself to this knowing.

There are a number of important themes in this dialogue: the impact of distrusting one's inner knowing, the experience of dissolution, the discovery of an abiding sense of being, and the opening of a powerful descending current of energy. Carol recognized that her tendency to discount her deeper knowing was an attempt to hold on, be in control, and stay safe. Her self-doubt was a form of resistance.

As she trusted what she knew to be true, that it was safe to open to her core aliveness, her system opened up. This opening initially brought a sense of dissolution and nausea, a disorientation. She was terrified that she would lose herself. When she could acknowledge to herself that she was still here—*Here I am. Nothing happened to me*—her fear diminished. As our ordinary identity falls away like a set of old clothes, the sense of "I am" remains.

When Carol asked herself if she could let herself know what she knew, she felt an energy stream down her legs and pour out through the bottoms of her feet. She wondered if her body could expand and allow this influx. It takes a while for our body to adjust to a higher vibrational frequency as we open to our true nature. This energetic dimension of awakening and embodiment is usually not explicitly described in spiritual literature because it happens below the level of conscious awareness.

As we recognize and surrender to our deepest knowing, our body undergoes a process of transformation. Since the body is fundamentally a field of vibration, it up-levels and clarifies as we come out of the illusion of separation. The process is similar to cleaning a dull, muddy window and discovering beautifully stained glass beneath, a translucent portal of light with a unique coloration.

Toward the end of our conversation, I sensed that the grip at the base of Carol's spine had relaxed and that a powerful descending current of energy was unfolding. This is a common experience as the energy center at the base of the spine opens. After spending decades in an inner clench that drove her attention up into her head, inducing hypervigilance and unnecessary thought (remember the image of a submarine's long periscope in chapter 8?), Carol was beginning to relax, trust herself, and land in the present moment. What is this downpouring of energy that Carol called the "river of life"? After guiding both individual and group work with thousands of people, I've observed that there are two spontaneous and complementary currents of life energy. One descends and the other ascends.

The descending current has a grounding effect. As we open to it, we inhabit our body more fully. We can sense both a vertical and horizontal expansion. We find ourself landing in the here and now. Yet the "here" is more HERE, and the "now" is more NOW. In other words, we experience a nonlocalized here and a timeless now. The overall effect is that we open to our life as it is (more on these important themes in chapters 14 and 15). As a side note, Carol was afraid that she would be "swallowed by the ground" if she let herself land. This was a projection of her childhood terror of being engulfed by her dominating father, a theme we visited in the prior chapter. Rather than being engulfed, however, she was discovering for the first time as an adult that it was safe to inhabit her body.

The ascending current of life, sourced in pure potentiality, arises from the hidden depths of the ground. It feels like a vibrant spring of life energy that spontaneously wells up and pours out through us. Interestingly, the more we inhabit our body, the stronger this upwelling, creative life energy becomes. I think of this as the animating life current. It is very powerful and nonpersonal. Interestingly, this is what I felt so strongly as I sat with Rob as he died. I was experiencing a release of consciousness from form, a transcendent movement. It felt as if life was continuing on to a higher level.

At the end of our conversation, I encouraged Carol to give herself to her knowing. When we do this, it becomes increasingly difficult to distinguish life from death. They are flip sides of the same thing, both expressions of the unknown. When we resist one, we resist the other. As a result, when we are willing to "die before we die," we are also willing to fully live while we are alive.

11

Falling Open

The bad news is there's no parachute.
The good news is there's no ground.

—(often attributed to) Chögyam Trungpa Rinpoche

I n this chapter we will explore the experience of letting go and falling open as our false ground dissolves. This is such an important
part of the process to describe because once we leave our familiar
ground of separation and illusory control, we open to a fathomless
depth and dark mystery.

About ten years ago on Father's Day, my son James and I drove
out to a small airport in the central valley of California to tandem-
parachute out of a small plane from ten thousand feet. I was interested
in the experience of free-falling. After we signed our liability waivers

in case of death, we met our young South American instructor. He was covered with tattoos, wore multiple earrings, and radiated a thrill-seeking vibe. In his thickly accented English, he gave us the instruction to "make like banana" when we fell out of the plane strapped to the back of our instructor. He showed us a drawing of a large upturned yellow banana and grinned. End of orientation.

Half an hour later, as I leaped out of the plane, securely attached to the back of an instructor, I was at first surprised by the volume of the wind shear in my helmet. After a few seconds I relaxed into the experience of free-falling and arched my back like an upturned banana as we hurtled toward the earth at 120 miles an hour. It was great. There was nothing to do, just relax into the fall and let gravity do its work. After about thirty seconds, the instructor pulled a cord and the parachute popped open, jerking us suddenly upward before we settled into a gentle descent overlooking almond orchards and farmlands for miles around. A few minutes later we floated gently to the ground like a milkweed blossom.

While I enjoyed my free fall, it was a pale version of what it can sometimes feel like when our familiar ground gives way to a feeling of groundlessness. The skydiving metaphor is somewhat misleading because it suggests that we fall endlessly through space as a separate self. The experience is more that, as the sense of vast space opens up below our body, we discover that we *are* this spacious underground awareness.

This downward opening parallels the opening behind our body that happens when the back of the heart area opens.[1] This process of unfolding spaciousness—whether above, behind, or below—is more like a house that is being dismantled. First the roof, then the walls, and finally the foundations come off. What is revealed in this deconstructive process? We are open, empty space in all directions—global space.

Sometimes this descent is precipitous, a bumpy ride down a steep slope through a series of trapdoors. Other times the process is gentler and more gradual. The latter has been true for me. For years it has felt as if an invisible force has been drilling down through the bedrock of my instinctual conditioning, slowly releasing fixations and trapped energy and opening up a groundless ground. It is as if I made some unconscious decision to get to the bottom of everything. It turns out that the "bottom of everything" is open.

Whether sudden or gradual, we often feel like we're falling when our inner grip of control relaxes and this underground space opens up. We are releasing our deeply held illusion of control. We realize that, try as we might, we've never been running the show. Stuff just happens. Our steering wheel was illusory. We thought we were the doer and the chooser. Indeed, doing has been happening and apparent choices have been made, but despite appearances, there has never been an individual entity that was doing or choosing anything. Something unimaginably greater has been running the show. It is our job to listen to and consciously cooperate with this deeper current of life. It is a radically different way to live.

We are invited to let go and trust, to surrender our willfulness. In religious terms, our one prayer is "Thy will be done." According to Meister Eckhart, the great fourteenth-century Christian sage, "A man should never pray for any transitory thing: but if he would pray for anything, he should pray for God's will alone and nothing else, and then he gets everything."[2] It is important to note, though, that even when the heart awakens to our essential oneness, a residual level of willfulness remains. A profound emotional opening doesn't automatically transpose to the instinctual level. The release of the heart-knot of separation doesn't necessarily touch the existential grip in our guts. An entirely different level of seeing through and letting go is being asked of us, an even deeper descent and opening.

This phase of letting go can sometimes feel like we are standing on the edge of a cliff. If we jump or fall, will we be held? Have you ever heard about, watched, or perhaps even experienced one of those group trust-building exercises where you close your eyes, fall backward, and let yourself be caught by others? In a similar way, we wonder if life will hold us if we inwardly let go. This morning, just before I began writing this chapter, I had an online session with someone who experienced the dissolution of a very subtle layer of this underground contraction. He described his experience as "falling into being held." We can't fully know this sense of being held until we experience it firsthand.

When we stop gripping ourself, we allow ourself to be held. Have you ever floated in temperate salt water? Every summer, when the shallow waters of Tomales Bay along the Northern California coast have warmed sufficiently, my wife, Christiane, and I swim there. Mostly I enjoy floating effortlessly on my back for minutes at a time, dissolving into the sky and water. The sense of being held is somewhat like this—our whole body relaxes and opens as we feel buoyed by something greater.

However, as I noted in chapter 8, if we grew up never really feeling held, it will take more time for this sense to unfold. If that's true for you, it may be helpful to sit in silence with someone you trust and feel cared for and open to the experience of being received just as you are. You can also relax into the experience of being physically held, if that is available.

When we feel met and attuned with in this emotional and energetic way and truly let this experience in, our system relaxes and realigns. As we've discussed already, we are deeply relational beings that need to feel physically, emotionally, and energetically held, especially when we are young. So, as we feel our false ground dissolving, these unresolved childhood needs will inevitably surface in order to be met. It doesn't mean we have to become dependent upon others. Letting ourself be held is a temporary step to our true autonomy.

Sometimes an archetypal figure such as the Great Mother will appear in a dream or deep meditation. In Western cultures she often appears as the Virgin Mary, even to non-Catholics and non-Christians. Sometimes she appears as an ancient goddess, taking on a more pagan and earthy form. If she does appear, be like a child and relax into her loving embrace. Amma, the famous "hugging saint" from India, embodies this archetype. I spent some time with her the first few years she came to the United States in the mid to late 1980s.

She would take thousands of us, one by one, into her arms and whisper, "Ma, ma, ma" into our ears. Despite having a loving mother and wife, I could sense that her intimate whispers touched some deep place in my psyche that had never been met.

Ultimately there is not someone being held and someone or something that holds us. There is just a sense of surrender. The separate wave relaxes into the ocean of Being. As we recognize the futility of struggling, a letting go happens. On some level, most of us believe that we will only be safe if we hold ourself in a tight grip. This isn't true. When we see this in a deep way, there's a spontaneous letting go. We don't try to let go; it happens on its own. It is enough that we are willing to sincerely investigate.

"There's Nothing to Hold On To"

In the following exchange, Riyaz shares his experience of sitting with an online partner who slowly and, with appropriate pauses, repeatedly asked him, "What is the deepest nature of the ground?" In this case, the inquiry is into the nature of the ground that we are letting go into rather than the one that wants to be safe. Upon hearing the question, Riyaz immediately experienced a trapdoor opening that led, at first, to a dramatic and very disorienting experience of free-falling.

Riyaz: As soon as the question [What is the deepest nature of the ground?] was asked in the dyad, a trapdoor opened up and [there was] just a free fall. I gave myself to it. There was an incredible amount of disorientation, nausea, shakiness. Eventually I started to feel a contraction in the solar plexus. That's where the nausea was. I started to breathe and the body started to move. Breath started to happen, and I started to unwind. I felt more verticality and an upward current like a serpent. I just wanted to give attention to this. It feels like this has been happening for a while. The shock and disorientation of it was so powerful. There's some residual experience here that I just wanted to share with you.

John: Good. This is a kind of archetypal movement, the archetype of the trapdoor [*laughs*]. I don't know if there's such an archetype; I'm making that up. We discover that what we took to be our ground is not, and a release happens. There's a deconstruction of our false ground and then an opening. I say archetypal because this letting go is such a common process. At first there's disorientation. We've oriented to some kind of ground that falls away. So we become disoriented and nauseous. The control center is in the solar plexus. We wonder [*makes turbulent sound and movement with hands*], *What's happening here? How do I stay in control?*

Riyaz: Yeah. It was so clear that there was nothing to hold on to.

John: That's right. Nonetheless, the system is reorienting.

Riyaz: There's something gripping, isn't there?

John: Yeah. Something's gripping that's unconscious, even though there's a deep sense of surrender. The system initially disorients and then reorients to our infinite nature. We discover on a bodily felt-sense level that we are not the finite creature we've taken ourselves to be. We are the infinite having a finite experience. [*Pause*] That can be a little disorienting. [*Chuckles*]

Riyaz: Actually, that feels very orienting when you say that. And yet I'm still aware of this—it doesn't feel nauseous right now—swirling in the solar plexus.

John: Just allow and be with that. It's part of the unwinding.

As our conventional ground dissolves, it is common for a somatic contraction and feeling of nausea to localize in the solar plexus. As I noted in chapter 8, this is the energy center that governs our attempt to be in control. Despite giving himself fully to the inquiry, some part of Riyaz was resisting a natural letting go. As he began to breathe, his body started to move and unwind residual tensions. It is important to allow our body to spontaneously move when this release happens. It can feel like we are a snake shedding an old skin. The body is throwing off a hard shell and softening a rigid core. Usually these movements are gentle, but occasionally the shaking is more intense, especially when traumatic material is releasing. These episodes usually pass quickly and are completely beneficent.

As this release progressed, Riyaz experienced a growing sense of verticality, the felt-sense of his body expanding along a vertical line above the head and below the feet. This sense of being vertically aligned is a common sign of being in touch with one's inner knowing.[3] We often sense this when we are coming into alignment with ourself, inwardly lining up and lighting up. This relates to the awakening of the central channel of energy along the spine. Interestingly, Riyaz described experiencing this upward current of energy as being "like a serpent," a traditional symbol of kundalini.

It is important to note the spontaneous nature of this energetic opening. Riyaz was not trying to manipulate energy. The sense of verticality and a serpentlike upwelling current were the by-products of a natural unfolding. As deep contractions unwind, energy is freed and our body naturally finds a more easeful and upright posture. While it is very helpful for us to attune with our body, it can be tricky if we are trying to willfully manipulate subtle energies. Our conscious mind rarely understands the best way for our body-mind to unfold. If we are intentionally directing subtle energies, it is important to have an attuned, experienced guide.

At the time of this meeting, it wasn't clear what Riyaz's gripping was about. In the year or two that followed, he uncovered and worked through both a survival terror of starvation inherited from his Indian ancestors as well as an experience of abandonment during his early infancy, both of which partially obscured clear access to his deepest ground. His love of truth eventually led him to and through this difficult conditioning.

In our exchange, I suggested that he was undergoing a profound reorientation to his infinite nature and that this could be disorienting. In fact, he felt oriented hearing this reflection. Something in him knew that it was true. By this point, his nausea had dissolved. It was enough for him to trust and allow the further unwinding. There was nothing to hold on to and nothing that he needed to hold on to.

This is a deep experiential insight that radiates through our whole body-mind system. There is nothing to grasp and nothing to push away. When we really get this, our argument with reality ends.

Once we've worked through our psychological and existential resistance and let ourselves fall open, what is the nature of the ground we are opening to? And what is the impact of this ground-level opening? We'll be exploring these questions for the remainder of the book. Carl Jung will be our guide into the collective unconscious in the next chapter. But before we join him on his remarkable, groundbreaking inner journey, I invite you to sit with the question that Riyaz was pondering. Discover what it evokes for you. It's one of my favorites.

Inquiry
What Is the Deepest Nature of the Ground?

Find a place where you won't be disturbed. If possible, sit comfortably upright with your feet on the ground. Close your eyes and take several slow, deep breaths. (*Pause*)

Remind yourself that there's no problem to solve, nowhere to go, and nothing to get. Allow your attention to drop down and into the core of your body. (*Pause*)

Once you've settled in, ask yourself, *What is the deepest nature of the ground?* Let go of the question and be quietly receptive. (*Pause*)

Gently pose this question several more times and be open. (*Pause*)

Let in a response in any form—a belief, an image, a felt-sense, or a direct knowing. (*Pause*)

Take as much time as you'd like. Be sure to let in any insights or shifts.

Take your time transitioning back to normal activity. Notice if the ground feels any different to you during the day.

12

Carl Jung's Underground Journey into the Collective Unconscious

The difference between most people and myself is that for me the "dividing walls" are transparent . . . the world has from the beginning been infinite and ungraspable.

—Carl Jung, *Memories, Dreams, Reflections*

Two nights ago I had the following dream: I am standing inside a large house with a number of spacious, minimally furnished rooms. I am holding Carl Jung's oversized, illustrated *The Red Book* beneath my arm as I look for a place to settle in. I choose a room, put down the book, and briefly leave. Soon after, I return to find that someone is forming a class there. As I pick up my book and leave, I notice Brian, a Jungian analyst and longtime colleague of mine who had died earlier this year, standing in the hallway. He is beaming a beautiful smile as his longtime partner, Scott, stands smiling next to him. I am very happy to see that Brian is doing so well and suspect that I must be at the Jung Institute in San Francisco. As another empty room fills for a seminar, I head outdoors onto a grassy area where an even larger study group is forming to my left. I head off toward a shady area in the distance on the periphery of the lawn. Once I sit, Carl Jung quickly approaches and stands immediately behind me. He starts softly playing a guitar. I don't hear the music so much as feel it. My body starts swaying back and forth, resonating with the inaudible, harmonious sound. I feel a deep sense of well-being.

Clearly my psyche was getting ready to approach this chapter about Jung. It's noteworthy that I had to leave the Jung Institute's building and go outside to the periphery of the lawn in order to meet Jung himself; it did not happen within the institute or a group but rather on the edge of the property. It is also significant that he stood behind me and that we connected via nonverbal attunement, considering Jung wanted people to discover their own path to wholeness and not blindly follow his teachings. On several occasions he was known to have exclaimed, "Thank God I am not a Jungian!"[1]

This attunement with Jung is recent. Our rendezvous began over two years ago when I first started writing this book. At the time, I had written a much too lengthy introduction and was beginning chapter 1 when a quiet inner voice said, *Stop*. So I did. Something was unclear. I realized I needed to revisit Jung's groundbreaking encounter with the collective unconscious. If I was to write in depth about the multidimensional ground, ranging from our personal ground to the groundless ground, I needed to include the subtle and extremely potent strata that he had so courageously unearthed. I also needed to become more intimate with it within myself. It felt like the book was writing me as much as I was writing it. My inner guidance was directing me to more fully surrender to this process.

As a result, I reread his remarkable memoir *Memories, Dreams, Reflections*, published in 1961, which had made such an impact on me when I was in graduate school. I also dove into his *The Red Book*, published in 2009, that intimately describes his confrontation with the unconscious that began in 1913 and continued for many years. Jung was understandably hesitant to publicly share this part of his journey while he was alive, given its raw and prophetic form. The two books form a complete circle, a kind of mandala, detailing the initial eruption of an incandescent "stream of lava" that radically reshaped his life in his late thirties to his final reflections in his eighties. He lived an amazing life and left a vast body of work that arguably impacted Western culture more than any other twentieth-century psychiatrist or psychologist, including his mentor Sigmund Freud.

If we are sincere in our desire to open to the ground, we must include Jung's discoveries of the collective unconscious. Any genuine descent will, at some point, encounter this domain. Few have mapped it so intimately and thoroughly.[2] However, before we explore this terrain, it is important to know more about Jung himself.

Jung had an exceptionally porous psyche. As the opening quote suggests, what were dividing walls for others were for him, from the earliest age, transparent. At age three, in the first dream he remembers, he descended down a stone-lined staircase and discovered an enormous underground room with a mysterious throne upon which stood an enormous phallus-like object with a single eye. Between the ages of seven and nine, he vigilantly tended a sacred fire in the spaces of an old wall in his garden. He would sit upon a nearby stone and play an imaginary game:

> I am sitting on top of this stone and it is underneath. But the stone could also say "I" and think, "I am lying here on this slope and he is sitting on top of me." The question then arose: "Am I the one who is sitting on the stone, or am I the stone upon which he is sitting?" This question always perplexed me, and I would stand

up, wondering who was what now. The answer remained totally unclear, and my uncertainty was accompanied by a feeling of curious and fascinating darkness.[3]

When Jung was twelve, he realized he was actually two different people: a schoolboy in the 1880s as well as an important old man who lived a hundred years before. These gradually developed into what he called his personalities: No. 1, "the spirit of the times"; and No. 2, "the spirit of the depths." The first was rational and contemporary, while the second was intuitive, instinctual, historic, and ultimately timeless: ". . . above all close to the night, to dreams, and to whatever 'God' worked directly in him."[4] His life was spent mediating these two sides—the one who sat upon the stone and the stone itself—that he felt were in everyone:

> The play and counterplay between personalities No. 1 and No. 2 which has run through my whole life, has nothing to do with a "split" or dissociation in the ordinary medical sense. On the contrary, it is played out in every individual. In my life No. 2 has been of prime importance, and I have always tried to make room for anything that wanted to come to me from within.

When Jung was fourteen, he had a glimpse of nondual reality when he visited a distillery and sampled the liquor.[5]

> I was wafted into an entirely new and unexpected state of consciousness. There was no longer any inside or outside, no longer an "I" and the "others," No. 1 and No. 2 were no more; caution and timidity were gone, and the earth and sky, the universe and everything in it that creeps and flies, revolves, rises, or falls, had all become one. I was shamefully, gloriously, triumphantly drunk.

I accent this particular experience because of the clear nondual signature; there was no inside or outside, no separate parts, and no self and other. While Jung apparently had easy access to this undivided consciousness, at least as a boy and adolescent, it was never the main focus of his life's work. Instead, he was inexorably drawn to explore and consciously express "the spirit of the depths," personality No. 2. This became his life's work, his dharma.

Jung's Descent

When Jung broke from Freud in 1912, he became unmoored from his rational personality No. 1, which had predominated in his work as a psychiatrist. He decided to start over from scratch. In order to reconnect with his childhood inner life, he built a whole village out of small stones. His early imaginal life reawakened and quickly turned into a flood. In October 1913, while traveling by train, he was overpowered by a waking-state vision of a monstrous sea of blood engulfing northern Europe. He experienced the same vision more vividly two weeks later, but this time with an inner voice that said, "Look at it well; it is wholly real and it will be so. You cannot doubt it."[6]

Jung feared that he was becoming psychotic. When World War I broke out in August the following year, he began to realize that he was tapping into a larger, collective field. During this tumultuous period, he reported often feeling helpless and fearful, as if giant blocks of stones were falling on him; sometimes he would grip his table to steady himself. He took careful notes of his inner experiences as he began this "voluntary confrontation with the unconscious."[7] To fully open, he knew he needed to let himself plummet down. In December 1914, he wrote, "I resolved upon the decisive step. I was sitting at my desk once more, thinking over my fears. Then I let myself drop. Suddenly it was as though the ground literally gave way beneath my feet, and I plunged down into the dark depths."[8]

After this, he "frequently imagined a steep descent. I even made several attempts to get to the very bottom. The first time I reached, as it were, a depth of about a thousand feet; the next time I found myself at the edge of a cosmic abyss. It was like a voyage to the moon, or a descent into empty space . . . I had the feeling that I was in the land of the dead."⁹

When he reached this depth, he initially encountered two figures: an old man who called himself Elijah, and a young blind girl named Salome. Soon Elijah, a biblical prophet, transformed into Philemon, who Jung described as "a pagan . . . with a Gnostic coloration." For Jung, Philemon was an entirely distinct entity, an inner guru and prophetic wise man who knew things that Jung did not.

In early 1916 Jung had one of his strangest experiences. One day at 5:00 pm his doorbell frantically rang as his house seemed to fill with ghostly entities. He and others in his house could hear the doorbell ringing, and he could see the doorbell moving, but no one was there. Then he heard an inner chorus of voices cry out, "We have come back from Jerusalem where we found not what we sought."¹⁰ This is when the strange *Seven Sermons to the Dead* flowed out of Jung for three days, as if written by Philemon. Once Jung started to write, the haunting ended.

This descent and opening was the defining moment of Jung's life. He was establishing a conscious relationship "to the collectivity of the dead; for the unconscious corresponds to the mythic land of the dead, the land of the ancestors . . . the voices of the Unanswered, Unresolved, and Unredeemed."¹¹ From then on, his life was no longer his alone. It "belonged to the generality." He dedicated his life to the psyche; all of his future work came from this creative upwelling:

> The years when I was pursuing my inner images were the
> most important of my life—in them everything essen-
> tial was decided. It all began then; the later details are
> only supplements and clarifications of the material that
> burst forth from the unconscious, and at first swamped
> me. It was the prima materia for a lifetime's work.¹²

All of Jung's subsequent theoretical formulations arose out of this lavalike flow: the persona/shadow, anima/animus, archetypes, the conjunction of opposites, the collective unconscious, the individuation process, synchronicity, and the Self. More than two decades after this initial eruption, Jung traveled to India.

Jung and Ramana Maharshi

When Jung visited India in 1937, he was familiar with the teachings of Ramana Maharshi through his colleague, the German Indologist Heinrich Zimmer. He could have easily visited the great sage when he was in Madras. Instead, he chose not to:

> I studiously avoided all so-called "holy men." I did so because I had to make do with my own truth, not accept from others what I could not attain on my own. I would have felt it as a theft had I attempted to learn from the holy men and to accept their truth for myself.[13]

Yet Jung's reluctance to see Ramana was rooted in more than just wanting to come to his own truth. After all, genuine teachers support this in their students. He also resisted Ramana's specific teachings about the nature of the self and spiritual realization, which he viewed as too one-sided. Upon returning from India, Jung expressed his doubts in a foreword to Heinrich Zimmer's book about Ramana's teachings that was later entitled "The Holy Men of India":

> I simply could not, despite the uniqueness of the occasion, bring myself to visit this undoubtedly distinguished man personally. For the fact is, I doubt his uniqueness: he is of a type that always was and will be. Therefore it was not necessary to seek him out.
>
> Shri Ramana's thoughts are beautiful to read. What we find here is purest India, the breath of eternity, scorning and scorned by the world. It is the song of the ages, resounding like the shrilling of crickets on a summer's night, for a million beings. This melody is built upon the

one great theme, which, *veiling its monotony* [emphasis added] under a thousand colorful reflections, tirelessly and everlastingly rejuvenates in the Indian spirit, whose youngest incarnation is Shri Ramana himself.[14]

He believed that Ramana, like every Indian guru before him, taught that only Brahman, stainless pure awareness, was real and that the ego was an illusion to see through and dissolve. Jung thought this approach depreciated and abolished the body and individual consciousness. He wrote that visiting a man who was only holy and wise interested him as much as seeing a rare dinosaur's skeleton!

In essence, Jung put Ramana in a generic frame and discarded him. This attitude is shocking to those who knew Ramana firsthand. I had a taste of Ramana's presence when I visited his ashram in 1988, nearly forty years after he had passed. I felt a palpable presence in the small hall where he had given darshan for many years. I also meditated alone for several hours in one of his caves on the side of Arunachala and intuitively understood why he considered the mountain to be his guru and an embodiment of Shiva. While there, I clearly sensed an enormous pillar of light—a potent, radiant verticality. Did Jung, who was so attuned to archetypes, avoid an ego-threatening encounter with Ramana? If so, he never mentioned it.

Jung's focus was clearly elsewhere. He was fascinated by the "insane contradiction" between existence in the cosmic Self and the "amiable human weakness" to root into the black earth: "For how else can one perceive the light without the shadow, hear the silence without the noise, attain wisdom without foolishness?"[15]

Jung did meet a humble householder disciple of Ramakrishna who he greatly admired:

> My man—thank God—was only a little holy man, no radiant peak above the dark abysses, no shattering sport of nature, but an example of how wisdom, holiness, and humanity can dwell together in harmony, richly,

pleasantly, sweetly, peacefully, and patiently without limiting one another, without being peculiar, causing no surprise, in no way sensational. . . . He has found meaning in the rushing phantasmagoria of Being, freedom in bondage, victory in defeat.[16]

Jung believed that the path of individuation was an ongoing process of compromise and balance between the ego and the Self, the latter which he defined as the totality of the conscious and unconscious.[17] For Jung, the goal of life was a heightened and broadened capacity for reflection and a deepening relationship with the unconscious rather than a spiritual awakening.[18] This is why he preferred his "little holy man" who seemed to reconcile his ordinary and spiritual lives without appearing to be special in any way. Jung thought this humble disciple of Sri Ramakrishna (who he mistook as a disciple of Ramana) had surpassed his master in wisdom.

Unlike Ramana Maharshi, who accented discovering pure consciousness through self-inquiry, Jung focused on uncovering and integrating the deepest *contents* of consciousness, which had erupted like a volcano in 1913 and turned his life upside down. He was pioneering a different path, one he felt was more appropriate for Westerners.

Instead of attuning with an underlying silence and stillness, Jung was interested in actively evoking and engaging with the collective unconscious. This inspired his method of active imagination, where he would suspend critical attention, focus on a mood, and "become as conscious as possible of all fantasies and associations."[19] This process evoked myths or primordial images with which one would dialogue. Jung hoped this dialogue would gradually allow the birth of a new God image within one's soul as well as a new worldview that a soulless society desperately needed.

Jung clearly warned against identifying with these primordial images or archetypes, which he believed could lead to extreme states of inflation or deflation. To this point, when Jung was dialoguing with his "soul" in 1922, it encouraged Jung to proclaim a new religion:

"No one knows it as you do. There is no one who could say it as well as you do."[20] Instead, Jung created a new psychology. Even though Jung was a mystic at heart (personality No. 2), he needed to present his revelations to society as a scientist (personality No. 1). Jung was, above all, interested in the transformation of society as a whole and therefore presented his intuitive discoveries in the language of empirical science.

The Collective Unconscious and the Ground of Being

If Jung was interested in opening to and integrating the deepest currents of the ocean, nondual teachings emphasize opening and surrendering to the ocean floor. Thus, Jung focused on archetypes and Ramana Maharshi focused on the ground of awareness. While Jung advocated active imagination as a way to engage with the collective unconscious, Ramana encouraged a silent inquiry into and abidance in and as the unbounded sense of "I." Which is more important?

You will need to consult your deepest knowing to find out what is true for you. The response may change over time. Clearly Jung was compelled to follow his own path despite his exposure to nondual teachings. For Ramana, there was a clarion call to follow a spontaneous inquiry when he feigned death at the age of sixteen, asked himself "Who dies?" and awoke from the separate self as if from a dream.[21]

It is important to acknowledge the value of each approach and also see that they are not exclusive. In my in-depth work with people over four decades, I have observed a spontaneous interplay between these levels. At times our attention is drawn to our unresolved personal conditioning; other times to collective levels that we carry from our ancestors whose voices remain "Unanswered, Unresolved, and Unredeemed"; and other times to silent presence. That said, it is clear that this intuitive process of healing, growth, and awakening is greatly facilitated by consciously accessing our deepest ground of silent, open, and loving awareness.

It is easy to fixate on a particular approach and stop listening moment to moment to our inner knowing. Some nondual spiritual teachers devalue or undervalue psychological work, either because they avoid this exploration within themselves or because they don't need it. One of my main teachers, Jean Klein, completely dismissed the value of such work, although he was mostly familiar with Freudian psychoanalysis at the time. This devaluing attitude is gradually changing as nondual teachers break from rigid patriarchal roles and become more vulnerable and better educated about the impact of trauma and early attachment styles, and recognize the role of unresolved conditioning in themselves and their students. As a result, they are able to either work with this conditioning more skillfully or make appropriate referrals to contemplatively oriented psychotherapists.[22]

What of Jung's critique of Ramana and nondual teachings? Do these teachings depreciate and abolish the body and ego as he feared? When properly understood, they don't. However, if misused, they can foster inner division and dissociation. The point of nondual teachings is to see through the apparent separate self and discover the undivided nature of reality. This does not mean annihilating the individual body-mind. It means freeing the body-mind from an exclusive identification with itself.

When we realize that we are not *just* this body-mind, we feel an enormous sense of relief, as if a heavy weight has been lifted. All of the executive functions of the mind—such as memory, discernment, and decision-making—continue as before. Similarly, our body is released from a core tension and functions more naturally. It takes a lot of energy to pretend we are separate from the whole of life. This energy is liberated as we see through the illusion of separation. We are freed to be our individual self, and we are far less concerned about conforming to social norms. Essential authenticity, knowing who we really are, supports our unique expression. Most Westerners, and Indians for that matter, are not going to be wearing a loin cloth or sitting in a cave for decades as Ramana did. That was *his* unique expression at that particular time in that particular culture.

So while, in my opinion, Jung exaggerated the dangers of a nondual approach, having not directly experienced a nondual teacher or silent meditation or inquiry practice himself, he did detect a potential pitfall: dissociation. The practice of disidentifying from our body and mind can be used to distance from life. If our life is too emotionally painful, we may want to leave our body and get as far away from it as possible. With this aversive motive, spiritual teachings and practices can be used like a drug. The result is that we inwardly distance from our experience and become more divided and numb. We then act out our suppressed parts—our shadows. The antidote to this tendency is self-honesty and vulnerability.

Jung was keenly interested in recovering the soul, which he felt Westerners had lost with their hyper-rationalism, and discovering a new God image that unified opposites. In one of his final books, *The Answer to Job*, which he wrote in a kind of fever, he hoped "the indwelling of the Holy Ghost, the third Divine Person, in man, (would bring) about the Christification of many."[23] Despite seeing this collective potential, at the very end of his life Jung was apparently quite pessimistic about the fate of humanity.[24]

Nondual teachings tend to dismiss or devalue the soul level of human experience. After all, isn't it enough to go beyond all images and stories and know oneself as whole and undivided from the totality of life? Why concern oneself with the so-called soul? Isn't this just another construct of the separate self? In my experience, both within myself and those I have worked with, the soul level does spontaneously and quite powerfully emerge from time to time. I experienced this when the numinous image of a rainbow bridge, the symbolic template of my life's work, appeared during a deep meditation in my twenties. There have been many other occasions as well, including the impulse to write this book. These upwellings have an archetypal feel to them—deep currents of life working through us, largely outside of conscious awareness. It is important that we neither fixate upon nor dismiss them. If we fixate upon and overidentify with them, we become prone to egoic inflation. But if we dismiss them, we resist the deep flow of life.

These levels—the collective unconscious and the ground of being—are complementary. When we open to our deepest ground, we make ourselves available to the whole of life, to what life is asking of us. Sometimes a deep current arises from this ground and moves us in an unexpected direction for the benefit of the whole, as it did with both Jung and Ramana.

Inquiry
What Is Life Asking of Me?

Find a place where you won't be disturbed. If possible, sit comfortably upright with your feet on the ground. Close your eyes and take several slow, deep breaths. (*Pause*)

Remind yourself that there's no problem to solve, nowhere to go, and nothing to get. Allow your attention to drop down and into the core of your body. (*Pause*)

Once you've settled in, ask yourself, *What is life asking of me?* Let go of the question and be quietly receptive. (*Pause*)

Gently pose this question several more times and be open. (*Pause*)

Let in a response in any form—a belief, an image, a felt-sense, or a direct knowing. (*Pause*)

Take as much time as you'd like. Be sure to let in any insights or shifts.

If a direction suggests itself, take steps to act upon it. Acting on our inner knowing strengthens our connection to it.

13

Groundless Ground

> With this and that I tried to keep the bucket
> together, and then the bottom fell out. Where water
> does not collect, the moon does not dwell.
>
> —Adachi Chiyono

As the story goes, one evening, Adachi Chiyono, an ardent female Zen practitioner in the thirteenth century, was carrying a wooden bucket filled with water. As she gazed upon the moon's reflection on the water's surface, the bottom of the bucket suddenly broke and the reflection disappeared. At this moment she attained enlightenment. In the Zen tradition, she wrote the above poem to commemorate this opening. She went on to become the first female founder and abbess of a Japanese monastery.[1]

This is a beautiful image to contemplate. Can you sense its power? How many ways have you tried to keep your metaphoric "bucket" together in order to sustain an inherently unstable image and identity of yourself that is like the moon's reflection upon the water? How have you subtly or not so subtly tried to prove your value or disprove your lack of value to others or, more importantly, to yourself? How would it be to not prove, disprove, or improve anything about yourself? What if, all of sudden, you were to see the utter and complete futility of your self-improvement project and the bottom fell out of your need to be someone? What if you were to realize that you were never defined or confined by any image or story? That you have no roof, no walls, and no foundation? That you are no one and no thing? This was Adachi's realization. The bottom of her bucket broke open to her groundless ground.

Ordinary words cannot capture this spontaneous recognition of being essentially roofless, wall-less, and floorless. So we use negations, metaphors, and paradox to hint at what is intimately known yet impossible to fully convey with thought: luminous darkness, dynamic stillness, vibrant silence, and groundless ground. I invite you to savor each of these paradoxical metaphors for a moment and sense if they resonate with some quiet inner knowing. If they do, you are joining in Adachi's realization that is also your true nature. Buckets can break open at any moment "where water does not collect."

The term *groundless ground* is pointing to what is prior to our egoic ground and even our archetypal ground. It is before our personal biography as well as that of our ancestors who collectively dwell in the land of the dead. It includes our earthiness and precedes it. When the bottom falls out, it is as if we fall all of the way *through* the earth *into and as* infinite space. There is just empty openness. Darkness. Silence. Stillness. No one and no thing. It is the end of all stories about anything. This may sound like annihilation, from the Latin root *nihil*, meaning "nothing." Yet it is not nothing. It is neither something nor nothing. All conceptual categories fail. Open, lucid awareness remains even as there is no one who is aware. This is true right now as you read these words.

This falling open is effortless and spontaneous. It happens on its own, always unexpectedly. We are walking along with our ordinary bucket of water reflecting a familiar moon and *whoosh*, the bottom falls out. One moment there is someone and the next there is no one. If we carefully observe our ordinary experience, we will see that there are micro-moments of the bottom falling open with each silent gap between thoughts, each end of an exhalation, and each night when we fall asleep. Jean Klein encouraged his students to inwardly disrobe from all of their temporary identities and be naked as they lie in bed awaiting la petite mort of deep sleep, something I continue to often practice.

In what sense can that which is groundless also be grounding? Isn't an endless free fall profoundly disorienting? As I suggested in chapter 11, it is not that we are a separate self plummeting endlessly through space. Rather, we recognize that we *are* this openness. The lens of separation widens; our viewpoint opens into a viewspace. The result is profoundly stabilizing. We open to the truth of who we really are: an inexpressible openness.

As our false bottom falls away, we encounter another apparent paradox (for all paradoxes are only in the mind): the qualities of stability and solidity. That which is most spacious is also most stable and solid. We normally associate stability and solidity with the earth. Yet the earth severely quakes at times, especially here in California, and in a few billion years it will be torched by our exploding sun, which is only one among billions of other suns and galaxies. Suns and their "Goldilocks" planets (not too warm, not too cold) come and go like the breath, all forms appearing and disappearing like Adachi's moon on the water.

This groundless ground is not private property. There is no owner around to claim it. Instead, it is the cosmic commons shared by all beings. It is our common ground, our home ground. It is not an interrelated or interdependent ground. That is, it is not the realm of separate selves relating to one another. It is not the sharing of the me and the you—the small "we" space. It is the recognition of our shared beingness, of that which is prior to the me and the you. It is before age, gender, race, class, or even species. It is before thought, memory, and time. It is what we see when we innocently gaze into the eyes of another and recognize ourself looking back, like a sacred mirror. It is our shared ground of beingness.

While at first the groundless ground may feel like a vast underground openness beneath the body, in reality it is not localized. It quickly reveals itself to be global, 360 degrees all around. The head, heart, and ground are different doorways into this same global awareness, each with their own essential qualities. When we discover this openness through the mind, there is clarity and infinite spaciousness. Through the heart there is wholeness, unconditional love, kindness, and gratitude for no reason. Through the ground there is spacious stability and solidity. Similarly, what was once always quietly in the background seems to come into the foreground of awareness. Then background and foreground disappear. So do inside and outside. The metaphor of the ground, whether below or behind, completely falls away. As the bottom falls out and we surrender to utter darkness and emptiness, we also discover a field of pure potentiality that is prior to existence. Adyashanti writes,

> The Ground of Being is the source and suchness of all existence. You can think of it as an infinite unmanifest potentiality. As the source of existence, the Ground of Being transcends existence thoroughly, and yet is the ever-present suchness of all, including this very moment as you encounter these words. Prior to, yet of Being and nonbeing, someone and no one, fullness and emptiness, understanding and ignorance, the Divine Ground is experienced as something like the . . . gaze of eternity intimately close yet timelessly abiding as the Ground of all experience and perception.[2]

The ground of being is both transcendent and immanent, remote and intimate, empty and full. In this chapter I accent emptiness—silence, stillness, and darkness. To the separate self this feels like death. In a way, it is. Adya observes that opening to the ground of being tends to evoke the greatest resistance because it requires "dislodging the ego structure from the center of one's experience."[3] He advises only sharing those practices that most directly dislodge egoic roots with those who are on retreat with an experienced teacher.

Let's pause here and take in the importance of this cautionary note: to be rooted in the ground of being, we must be uprooted from our core egocentricity. This requires facing our deepest resistance. Attuned support is often vitally important. Once this uprooting and decentering occurs, there is a "visceral feeling of rebirth."[4] (More on this in the final section of this book.)

Meditation

Opening to the Groundless Ground

Find a place where you won't be disturbed. If possible, sit comfortably upright with your feet on the ground. Close your eyes and take several slow, deep breaths. (*Pause*)

Remind yourself that there's no problem to solve, nowhere to go, and nothing to get. Allow your attention to drop down and into the core of your body. (*Pause*)

Sense your breath low in the belly and let your attention rest there. (*Long pause*)

Allow your next exhalation to completely empty out into the space beneath your body. Do not grasp for the in-breath. Let it come on its own. Feel yourself being breathed. (*Long pause*)

Relax into and as this underground emptiness at the end of each exhalation. (*Long pause*)

Let go of all thoughts and identities. Be naked and empty. (*Long pause*)

Allow yourself to rest in and as darkness, in and as silence. (*Long pause*)

Be willing to be no one, to be nowhere, to be outside of time, without a self or a world, as if in deep sleep but awake. (*Very long pause*)

Be sure to take plenty of time coming out of this meditation. Notice what happens when you first open your eyes and begin to move. Spend some quiet time in nature, if possible.

Part 3

EMBODYING SPIRIT

As we consciously descend and explore our personal and collective ground, it begins to open. The dissolution of our constructed ground unveils the groundless ground and global awareness. Our journey of emptying out the nonessential allows for a blossoming—a rebirth where we knowingly return to our home ground in and as awareness.

We find ourself landing HERE in the very center of our ordinary life. However, this "here-ness" is not localized. As we inhabit our body more fully, we are less confined to it. We discover that the body is more open and spacious than we ever imagined.

As the tight grip of illusory control releases, we feel a current of life welling up from the depths. As we anchor in silence, an essential aliveness radiates through us with increasing ease. We sense a quiet inner alignment and flow.

We take our seat in our inner authority with a quiet confidence, neither asserting nor denying our inner knowing. No one is special. No one is higher or lower. We all share the same ground and heart of awareness.

Chapter 14

Landing HERE

Be here now.

—Ram Dass, *Be Here Now*

I spoke with the spiritual teacher and psychologist Ram Dass only once. It was in February 1989 at the end of a gathering with Jean Klein on a ridge above Tiburon, north of San Francisco. Ram Dass lived in Marin County at the time and had come to hear Jean speak, perhaps for the first time. My late wife, Linda, had died a few weeks earlier, and I was feeling strangely light and peaceful. Knowing that Ram Dass often spoke about death and dying, I approached him outside after Jean's talk, and told him of my very recent loss and strange absence of grief. I could feel his warm, inviting presence.

"Had my anticipatory grief prior to Linda's death satisfied my need to grieve?" I asked.

He kindly shook his head. "No, it did not. Your grief will come soon," he replied.

I appreciated his simple and spontaneous response. And, of course, he was right. Even though I felt like I was being "here," as his iconic book *Be Here Now* had counseled, I was in an altered, elevated state that would soon pass. A tsunami of grief was waiting in the wings, and it descended in full force a few weeks later.

What is the experience of being here now? It is certainly not what we think! Where is "here" exactly? And when is "now"? As the false bottom of our self-construct dissolves, we find ourselves landing right HERE in the middle of our very ordinary life. I use capital letters because the experience of being here opens up. There is no question that I am here, yet the "I" is impossible to locate. HERE also is unbounded; we can't find where it ends. Similarly, when we carefully investigate the so-called present moment, it disappears. In fact, the experience of NOW is timeless. Thus, "being here now" is not only about being more aware of our immediate sensory experience as I thought when I first read Ram Dass's book over five decades ago. At the deepest level, it is about the recognition of the unbounded nature of being itself.

As we open to our deepest ground, we inhabit our body in a way that is hard for the mind to grasp and difficult to describe. It is not a flight into light; we are not hovering, dissociated, or avoidant. There is a deep sense of being at rest in the body and on the earth. There is an alert acceptance of life as it is in the moment. We are no longer trying to be somewhere or someone else. The body feels palpably open, fluid, and translucent. It is not the dense object that we imagined we once lived inside and owned. Rather, it feels like the body is in us as awareness and is also a vibrant expression of this awareness. It feels largely empty of inner tension yet full of life. It operates more or less within the laws of physics with all of its limitations and flaws, aches and pains, yet our relationship with it radically changes. It no longer confines or defines us. We continue to take good care of it, nourishing it, resting it, and taking it out for regular walks. We also know that one day it will pass and that this is not a problem. When the wave subsides, the ocean continues.

There are degrees that we can consciously inhabit our bodies. Usually this is a gradual, top-down, outside-in process. The more we disidentify from our limiting thoughts, reactive feelings, and somatic contractions, the more awake awareness infuses the body. As conditioning is released and the veils of identity are seen and seen through, attention increasingly drops down and in. The body becomes a more intimate, wakeful, and clear vessel of light.

Acclimation

Naturally, the body gradually acclimates to the light of awareness. Our body can handle only so much change at a time, or it becomes overwhelmed. If it is flooded, it short-circuits. This happened to me when I did intense Reichian breathwork in my midthirties. My body was too dense to handle the energetic charge at the time, and I experienced tetany where my fingers and hands went into an involuntary freeze and start curling up—a very unpleasant sensation. A similar process can happen when the body is suddenly and dramatically catapulted into higher vibratory levels. It needs to gradually up-level or it will overload. Premature awakenings of kundalini, while rare, demonstrate this. So does overuse of psychedelics.[1] Part of the body's awakening is concerned with uncovering and digesting trauma. Anyone who has done this work knows that it takes time for the body to adapt to these shifts. As this happens, it can feel like we are living in a house while it is being remodeled.

The body, like all living systems, is a more or less complex and coherent field of vibration. This may sound esoteric, but it is a commonsense experience. At various times we can feel brighter or duller, well or poorly attuned, more open or closed. Often after attending a retreat, we feel more expansive, clear, and uplifted for a while before sliding back into a familiar, though slightly shifted, default mode.

These shifts in mental and feeling states have their subtle somatic correlates. The body is also adjusting its frequency, largely below conscious awareness. This takes time.

Most of us live on the outskirts of our body, unaware of the potential for an interior luminosity and aliveness. I certainly did for years. As we discover our true nature, our body unveils itself on an energetic level. Those who are energetically sensitive can clearly experience this. Yet it happens whether we can sense it or not. Sometimes I feel it happening in my students before they do. In any case, we experience ourself landing in our life as it is with all of its beauty and challenges.

"Not in My Body, Yet Fully Embodied"

In the following exchange, Elona, a psychotherapist who was attending one of my online seminars, describes opening to the ground and feeling less boundaried but more embodied than ever before. She briefly wondered whether she could function from this awareness as a therapist and discovered that she could with greater spontaneity and intimacy.

Elona: This morning I was doing last week's meditation "Opening to the Ground." I didn't have emotion with this then, but there is now. Something happened like what you were describing. Just going deep into that opening, deeper than I've ever gone before, opening to the ground. There was this . . . there's not even a reference point. I felt and have been feeling all day this being less concrete, less boundaried, not in my body yet fully embodied at the same time.

John: Yes.

Elona: I wasn't afraid. And I functioned. I met with all of my clients all day, and there's been this joining, this less concrete way of being that was very differently allowing what arose in ways that I wouldn't have necessarily expected. There wasn't really attachment or fear. There's a little emotion now as I'm describing it. I haven't experienced it before. It felt like I was almost tripping. There's not a clear reference point. I can say it was like this or like that, but it felt very new.

John: Very new. It is. I'm tracking your experience and recognize it very clearly. You are more here than ever, but it is not here in the ordinary way. It's very interesting. I've been describing this as a landing here, but the here is nonlocal. So we really feel that we are embodied. You feel that, yet the body is not what we think it is. It is very open. We embody openness. We go all the way through the body. We are not going somewhere else. We're actually here more fully than ever. Is this making sense?

Elona: Absolutely. The nonlocal makes sense. Nonlocal yet more fully here.

John: Both are true. The less localized we are, the more here we are. It's even more intimate. There's a release happening here, Elona. Some old way of holding and identifying yourself that this opening to the ground is releasing. The only reference may be to some psychedelic experience, but "I'm not tripping," right? [*Chuckles*] I'm here.

Elona: There was a little question of "Can I function?" Yet everything functioned. I didn't feel like I had to manage it.

John: There's the point about agency or doership. "Can I function?" is not the right question. It is, "Does *it* function?" Yes, it functions quite well! Thoughts come, words come, and things get done but not with the ordinary sense of "I am managing things." You said some feeling was arising?

Elona: Just as I started describing this a few minutes ago, there was some emotion. I don't know what it was—a combination of relief and grief.

John: Interesting.

Elona: Not grief per se, some kind of arising of this sensation in the sharing of it. Like being met. Yes, thank you for getting this. You recognize this.

John: Absolutely. Right away.

Elona: Recognition, that's it. Oh, thank God, yeah.

John: It's helpful to have this unusual perception be received and met. It helps us trust it. It helps us validate our own experience and trust it. I'm wondering, how is it right now?

Elona: There's still this fluidity of nonlocal. There's not this condensed sense and yet very present.

John: Very present. That says it very well. [*Chuckles*] As much as we can put words to it. Does it feel natural?

Elona: It does, actually. I was going to say, "I don't know if it's familiar or not." I don't know. I don't really care. It does feel natural.

John: Anything else you notice about this or yourself right now?

Elona: There's more of a heart sense with it that I've felt all day. It's been very interesting being with clients and being in that being-ness and guiding people in a very different way from this. It was just whatever came in the moment. There was this grounding, vertical awareness, and being in the heart and just exploring whatever arose. It was not even them and us. It was whatever arose together.

John: Not even them or me.

Elona: Yeah. Being in this together and just allowing whatever unfolded. It was really sort of magical.

John: Yes. This is my experience, too. [*Chuckles*] There's a spontaneity, a naturalness, a heartfelt quality of love here.

Elona: All being held by whatever it is. Being held in the heart. We all felt that with each other.

John: It's shared, too.

Elona: Shared.

John: It's not just some individual state. We're tapping into something we all share. Beautiful. Thank you!

Elona: Thank you!

Elona resonated with the description of being nonlocal but more here. Although her experience was unfamiliar, it felt natural. Interestingly, a feeling of both grief and relief arose as she shared her experience with me; she felt received and understood. This way of being is usually buried in the depths of our heart, hidden from ourself and others. There is a hard-to-pinpoint grief about losing touch with it. There is also great relief when we regain contact and feel met by another as we do. It was important for Elona to have her experience recognized by me. It allowed her to recognize and trust it herself.

As we more fully explored her apparently paradoxical experience of not being in her body in a familiar way yet being more embodied, she described how it impacted her relationship with her clients. There was no longer a "me" and a "them." Instead, there was a shared sense of beingness and a natural unfolding that felt magical. When we land HERE with another, we discover a shared field of awareness and sense of flow. When we feel held by something greater, the heart feels safe to fully flower.

Inquiry
Landing HERE

Find a place where you won't be disturbed. If possible, sit comfortably upright with your feet on the ground. Close your eyes and take several slow, deep breaths. (*Pause*)

Remind yourself that there's no problem to solve, nowhere to go, and nothing to get. Allow your attention to drop down and into the core of your body. (*Pause*)

Ask yourself, *What is the experience of fully landing here right now?*

Don't go to your mind for an answer. Just notice what spontaneously arises and let it in. Sit with this question for as long as you'd like. Experiment with your eyes first closed and then opened. (*Long pause*)

Then take your time as you ease back into your daily life.

15

The Upwelling Current of Life

In this birth God streams into the soul in such abundance of
light, so flooding the essence and ground of the soul that it runs
over and floods into the powers and into the outward man.

—Meister Eckhart, *Meister Eckhart: Sermons and Treatises*

The emptier we are, the more we are filled with light. From the
perspective of the Christian mystic Meister Eckhart, when there
is an inner "birth," it is the Godhead that floods an individual's
essence and ground. From the perspective of Nondual Shaiva Tantra,
which flourished in India a millennium ago, the more we recognize
our true nature, the more Goddess Shakti (which was shorthand for
the light of awareness) pervades the central channel, the energetic core
of the body.[1] Tibetan Dzogchen teachings describe a core of radiant

consciousness within the body.[2] Whether it is from the Godhead, the Goddess, or our inherent Buddha Nature, when we open to the ground of being, we may experience a palpable influx of light and energy into the body-mind. A spontaneous energy wells up from the depths and lights up and aligns the interior of the body.

When I share this approach and understanding, I try to stay as close as possible to direct experience and not impose traditional theoretical frameworks. If these cross-cultural descriptions of spiritual awakening and transformation are accurate, we should be able to replicate them without believing or even knowing about them. This has been my experience. Nonetheless, it is interesting to discover that over many centuries and across diverse spiritual cultures, spontaneous openings to the ground have similar experiential markers. An upwelling current of life is one of them.

Several potential pitfalls arise as I describe subtle energy experiences that sometimes unfold as the depths of the ground opens. First, not everyone who opens to their deepest ground experiences this. We are all wired differently and have different sensitivities. Some people have profound and enduring openings without any awareness of subtle energetic shifts. Opening up does not require that we consciously experience energetic "fireworks." Second, it is very easy for the mind to fixate on particular experiences and mistake them for the source of those experiences: primal awareness. It is good to remember that all experiences are transient; they come and go. Don't be attached to them. Finally, we can easily identify with these energetic phenomena and use them to reinforce our spiritual ego: *Look how special I am!* This just adds another layer to our inner prison. Please keep these pitfalls in mind as you continue reading.

As the primal contraction at the base of the spine relaxes and releases, our energy field opens to the deep ground. Often we can feel a tingling in our legs and feet as this happens, as if the lower half of our body is coming alive. We can sense that we are connecting more intimately with our body as well as the earth. As this visceral connection develops, our trust in life grows. We feel more spacious and, at the same time, stable. It becomes increasingly easy to anchor into a profound silence, stillness, and darkness. At some point we realize that silence can sing, stillness can dance, and darkness can radiate light. In other words, our deepest ground is not nothing; it contains the potential for everything. Rather than being static, it is inherently dynamic. It is the source of an upwelling current of life.

We may experience this influx subtly or dramatically depending upon our sensitivity. For those who sense it, it is usually fairly subtle. As we become more in touch with our deepest nature, the sense of this current grows. We may visualize it as a growing interior light, sense it as a radiance and warmth in our core, or just feel lighter and more open. We may also feel more inwardly aligned as inner divisions spontaneously dissolve and disparate parts fall into place, a process of spontaneous harmonization.

As our core is suffused with this current, there is a growing sense of nonpersonal intimacy with all of life, what the Zen master Dogen and Chan masters before him called an intimacy with the "ten thousand things." We no longer feel that the world is something separate from us. It, too, is our body. Rather than viewing it as something to exploit, we intuitively know it is to be treasured. We feel like we are tapping into something that is shared by all living creatures and that animates all of life. As the interior fetters of identity fall away, it feels like our natural openness is shared by all of life. I can't assert that it *is* shared, for this is unknowable. But it certainly *feels* as if it is.

This upwelling life current also brings a sense of essential aliveness that feels natural, spontaneous, and independent from circumstances. That last point is particularly important because this aliveness differs from the ordinary stimulation that arises from contact with the environment. Our essential aliveness is inherent and autonomous; it is there regardless of our particular experience.

As we attune with this life current, we may sense that it radiates in a vertical line extending both far above and below our physical body. If we try to find a beginning or end to this verticality, we can't. It seems to extend between and mediate our underground and overhead dimensions, between form and formlessness, as if the two are mirrors of each other. We begin to realize that these polarities are distinct but not separate. Heaven and earth are not two.

"Waking Up, Down, and Out"

In the following online conversation, Katy experiences an upwelling from the ground into the heart, throat, and back of the head, and initially wonders how to be with this conditioning as it arises. She also notices how this upwelling movement is different from her old "up and out" approach to spirituality that she followed before meeting Adyashanti. I felt a palpable energy welling up from the ground as we talked.

Katy: In this particular meditation [from a few minutes ago in the meeting] the ground is open and has been pushing into the heart and is now in the throat and back of the head, and it no longer feels down, which is interesting because I was one of those up and out people until I met Adya and came down and in. It is now out and around like the circumference, like the dispersion of the campfire, but rather than being light it is the ground.

The question is, when you were talking about that vulnerability and resourcing with this spacious presence, it's happening all of the time even during conversations with people. Is there anything to do with the muckiness or old stuff that comes up in that ground?

John: No, other than welcome it without judgment and with curiosity and affection. This [process] will definitely stir up the mud, working through these very dense, often unconscious, levels of conditioning. So the attitude is one of receptivity, just allowing it to be.

As you talk about it, Katy, there's this upwelling quality to the ground. First there's an opening, an allowing, and then a downfalling, almost as if the bottom drops out. And then an upwelling happens. There is tremendous life energy, the energies of the ground beginning to imbue and suffuse the body-mind, often in a bottom-up movement. So it will come through the belly and the heart, up through the throat and head as well. And what feels initially localized as ground down there begins to feel more here [*motions horizontally and then vertically*] and then ultimately all around.

There's a beautiful symbol that encompasses this movement and reality, which is the tree of life. In the Celtic tradition there's an image of an oak tree with a sturdy trunk. The branches fan out to touch the ground. The roots go down and spread out and then rise up to touch the branches. For me this is a beautiful image of what we are growing into as a whole embodied human being.

So we trust the process. It is very dynamic. We open to it and it works us. We don't have to try to work it. We simply open and trust this movement. It will do its harmonizing. It will do its clearing. It will do its integrating. We are open to and trust that.

Katy: Because I've had so much work going up and out, dissociating from the body, this inclusivity of the body is now like the macrocosm.

John: Yeah, micro- and macrocosm.

Katy: It is so freeing and vital. It enlivens the cells.

John: It does. It enlivens the whole body. The world comes alive.

Katy: Yeah [*chuckles*].

John: As the body comes into its essential aliveness, we experience the world coming into its essential aliveness.

Katy: Thank you so much!

This conversation allows us to explore a very important issue: How does this bottom-up approach differ from Katy's earlier up-and-out approach to spiritual development? After all, isn't there an ascendant movement of energy and attention in both cases? While I don't know the specifics of Katy's prior orientation and practice, it sounds as if it had a strong transcendent emphasis. The goal was probably to disidentify from the body-mind and cultivate increasingly refined states of consciousness. The potential problem with such an approach is that it can dismiss or devalue the body and reinforce a subtle duality, even as its goal is ostensibly nondual. Often the actual result is that our body is devitalized and we become more of a detached or even dissociated witness to our experience, including all of our human relationships. I experienced this during the "transcendental" phase of my spiritual search in my twenties. Like Katy, I was overly "up-and-out."

With the "down-and-in," or imminent approach, we understand that the point of spiritual awakening is to embody it, for the light of awareness to suffuse and transform the deepest levels of human experience. Transcending our limited mental identity is an important first step. After waking "up" out of our stories and self-images, however, we need to wake "down."

When the process of embodying our spiritual understanding descends through the emotional and instinctual levels of the body and reaches the deepest level of the ground, there is a spontaneous upwelling of an essential life energy that suffuses and vitalizes the whole body, something that Katy was sensing. Increasingly we experience the body as a microcosm of life, a sacred expression of the whole. We can viscerally sense that spirit is imminent within form as well as transcendent of it. This is the phase of waking "out"—that is, when the ground of wakeful, loving awareness radiates out into our daily life like the warmth of a campfire or like a fountain of water showering its surroundings. The image of the Celtic tree of life, with its strong vertical core and branches and roots that fan out and touch one another, visually uniting the sky and the earth, also beautifully expresses this lived reality. The point is there is a natural movement for this loving awareness to share itself with others, free of any agenda. This sharing is a spontaneous outpouring.

Meditation
Opening to the Current of Life

Find a place where you won't be disturbed. If possible, sit comfortably upright with your feet on the ground. Close your eyes, and take several slow, deep breaths. (*Pause*)

Remind yourself that there's no problem to solve, nowhere to go, and nothing to get. Allow your attention to drop down and into the core of your body. (*Pause*)

Sense your breath low in the belly and let your attention rest there. (*Long pause*)

Allow your next exhalation to completely empty out into the space beneath your body. Do not grasp for the in-breath. Let it come on its own. Feel yourself being breathed. (*Long pause*)

Relax into and as this underground emptiness at the end of each exhalation. (*Long pause*)

Let go of all thoughts and identities. Be naked and empty. (*Long pause*)

Allow yourself to rest in and as darkness, in and as silence. (*Long pause*)

Be willing to be no one, to be nowhere, to be outside of time, without a self or a world, as if in deep sleep but awake. (*Very long pause*)

Be open to an upwelling current of life from the ground. Don't try to imagine or create any experience. Simply be open to a spontaneous and natural movement from the field of pure potentiality. (*Very long pause*)

Take as much time as you'd like with this meditation. When there is a sense of natural completion, ease into your day and pay attention to this interior sense of aliveness.

16

Taking Your Seat

What before seemed ordinary appears as an extraordinary
revelation, and mundane life becomes a source of endless
wonder, unveiling its ever-present radiant freedom.

—Christopher D. Wallis, *Tantra Illuminated*

Some years ago, I visited a Gothic cathedral in the west of
France. As I savored the darkened interior, silence, and soaring
heights of the vaulted stone ceiling, I came across a surprising and
deeply moving sight: a large, carved wooden chair with a strip of
gold carpet leading up to it, both illumined by a swath of morning sunlight from a distant window. The chair was simple, elegant,
empty, and filled with light, a beautiful symbol of our inner seat of
authority.

While this chair was created by a skilled artisan for a Catholic bishop centuries ago, each of us has a similar empty and illumined seat of authority within us that is based upon our profound and intimate self-recognition. This seat is not conferred by any outer authority; it wells up from within as a quiet knowing that is prior to ordinary thought. Since it is not attached to a belief or any particular point of view, it does not assert, deny, or justify itself. It arises moment to moment and is unconcerned with appearances or outcomes. It is the small and deeply still "voice" within that communicates itself most eloquently through silent presence. It also makes itself known through sensations, feelings, metaphors, intuitions, clear thought, and spontaneous physical movements. Though subtle, it is tangible; its authenticity rings true when we hear or sense it in ourself or in others.

This inner authority comes from authentic self-knowledge. When this unfolds, there are no sacred texts, crowns, robes, or holy oils that British coronation rituals, for example, employ to evoke divine authority. It is not an authority *over* anyone else. This natural authority arises when consciousness recognizes itself and we are stripped of our illusory identity as a separate self. When this happens, the ancient need to be seen and validated by others falls away. The mind is dethroned from its falsely elevated (or devalued) state of being the center of the universe; it relaxes into a natural humility (*humus* means "ground" in Latin) as it bows down to a deeper knowing that is rooted in the ground of being.

What is known? That you are unbounded, open, loving awareness. That you are whole and not separate from the totality of life. That you are a living mystery.

When you find your inner seat, you feel deeply settled and at ease in your body, on the earth, and as open awareness. This multidimensional seating is foundational; it supports the natural unfolding of your own life as well as the lives of others. Most importantly, it supports the full flowering of the heart. Prior to discovering our deepest ground and taking our seat, we guard our heart and only partially share it with a few others with whom we feel safe. This changes as we discover where our essential safety lies. As our deepest ground awakens, unfolds, and stabilizes, the universal dimension of the heart is free to fully blossom.

This primal grounding of the heart has enormous individual and collective consequences. It allows for a steady and powerful outpouring of love and wisdom into the world. This will look different for everyone, depending upon your gifts and inclinations. For some it will mean carefully tending the garden of your personal relationships—nurturing, supporting, encouraging, and uplifting those in your immediate circle. For others it will be expressed in your social roles as teachers, healers, artists, builders, entrepreneurs, social activists, benevolent warriors, or leaders. In every case, the effect will be life-giving. However humble our roles may appear and whatever our actions may be, an impersonal and intimate light will radiate out into the shared field. It is obvious that something greater than the "little me" is at work through us. When this happens, we feel well used.

"Standing on Nothing and Falling into Depthless Love"

John and I had met individually online for a handful of mentoring sessions over a period of two years before he attended his first retreat with me. During this time, he experienced a rapid unfolding of his heart and ground. After the retreat, I asked him if he would be willing to write a short summary of his experience. The following is his own, slightly edited, report:

> I went on silent retreat nearly eighteen months after John and I "landed" in the ground unexpectedly during an inquiry session. We had been steadily allowing this shift to soak in ever since, and it seemed that the process of trusting in that discovery was nearing a turning point.

It was apparent that something was about to "drop." I felt like a ripened piece of fruit, about to fall off the tree.

On our second evening together as a group, John led us through a meditative inquiry about meeting core limiting beliefs from our deepest knowing. I waited for a limiting belief to arise, and one eventually did: *It is not safe in this body.* There was an immediate recognition that this was the belief that had been challenged, threatened, and aroused by the work John and I had done over the previous year and a half. As we sat with our deepest knowing about the limiting belief we had chosen, my feeling of a lack of safety in the body dissolved. It was a felt-sense of release, expansion, and falling all at once. However, the sense of falling quickly shifted to one of floating; I was somehow suspended and grounded at the same time, standing on nothing.

The next day as I walked the grounds of the retreat center, I experienced a perceptual shift. It was as though I could sense the world springing into being from nowhere while simultaneously disappearing into the same nowhere. This birth and death is not sequential; it is concurrent. I sat and wrote my experience in the form of poetry.

A few moments later, as I continued to walk, I heard words I didn't recognize echoing in thought: *Gone, gone, everything has gone over.* I couldn't figure out what it meant, and decided to look it up on the internet when I returned to my room. To my surprise, these are the closing words to the Heart Sutra of Buddhism, which I had never read in its entirety before. I was only familiar with the famous passage "form is emptiness, emptiness is form." I took the time to read the whole sutra that day and found my experience expressed in words much more eloquent than these.

This shift of perception has remained since the retreat and continues to deepen. Interestingly, less than a month after the retreat, I was diagnosed with melanoma cancer for the second time in five years, this time in an invasive form. As I move into surgeries, tests, and a sense of the unknown that caused me to spiral into terror several years ago, this time I only feel the depthless love that is always here, always now, and always what we are at our core. It is causeless and without need of an explanation.

Following several individual meetings where John had experienced a significant release and opening in the heart area, we both sensed a palpable shift of attention from his heart to the ground. It was like being in an elevator that suddenly dropped multiple stories. His attention had been marinating there for eighteen months when he arrived at the retreat. One afternoon I led the whole group in a simple inquiry: "Be open to a core limiting belief. Once it has clarified, ask yourself, 'What is my deepest knowing about this?' and then let the question go. Don't go to your mind for an answer. Be open to whatever comes. Let it in."

It is not safe in this body bubbled up from John's depths. As this core belief around unsafety was seen through, there was an immediate release, accompanied by a feeling of falling and then floating. He felt like he was "standing on nothing." In fact, he *was* standing (and sitting) on no-thing. The bottom of his ground had fallen open. The next afternoon, he wrote the following poem titled "Untethered":

Everything is let go.
Hands on the clock, dates on the calendar,
endless myths of "somewhere else."
The arguments, wounds, desires, brokenness, attainments;
aches in the joints, cracks in the heart, terror in the belly;

A whispering wind, sunlight on leaves, perfume of the flower
    petals;
Trauma, violence, and rage;
Rising, elation, relief;
Solitude, grief, clinging.
It's all let go.
In the letting go It's held
closer than closer than closer still
In Openness beyond speech and Depth beyond definition,
wordless, Silent Intimacy.
Life bursts forth, Love born of Timelessness,
Existence untethered.
All is the same and All is new,
as Here and Now spring up from the dark
vibrant mystery of the Ground.
Friday afternoon erupts into song as
finches, yard tools, and wind chimes sing hymns to our
    Unnameable Embrace.

Although John did not identify as a Buddhist and had never read
the Heart Sutra, a version of its famous concluding lines arose in his
mind: "Gone, gone, everything has gone over."[1] Once John found
his seat, his heart was untethered. Importantly, this openheartedness
continued after the retreat when he faced a round of treatment for a
newly invasive melanoma, a life-threatening illness that had terrified
him only a few years before. This time John faced his illness with an
unshakable sense of well-being. There is no need to affirm or assert
any belief about safety or unsafety since the sense of being profoundly
grounded does not depend on thought; it is not a matter of faith.
Rather, it is based upon a spontaneous and visceral sense of knowing
that all is well, no matter what.[2]

Inquiry
Trusting and Following

I invite you to innocently sit with the following question from time to time: *How would my life change if I completely trusted and followed my inner knowing?*

I invite you to trust yourself and begin to act upon this knowing.

Conclusion

Open-Ended Embodiment

I envision this book as a user-friendly guide to embark upon an essential underground journey. It takes clarity, courage, and a deep love of the truth for you to undertake this exploration. If you have taken the time to carefully reflect on this material and try many of the meditations and inquiries, I commend you! I also invite you to keep exploring them. Deeper layers will reveal themselves as you do. I've tried to make this unfamiliar and often challenging terrain as accessible as possible. I hope these descriptions, reports, and practices help light the way. Consider this book as a pointer; take what's useful and ignore what's not. Your inner knowing is your best guide.

The most important factor for discovering your deepest ground is your love of truth. Of course, I am not referring to any dogma or belief system. I mean your essential nature as open, spacious, loving awareness that quietly awaits your conscious recognition. Our true nature is quietly calling all of us home.

This journey requires you to face and resolve significant challenges, especially your deepest personal and existential fears. It also yields the most precious gift: abiding self-knowledge. It differs from the classic hero or heroine's underground journey in several significant ways.

First, it is a journey of stripping away and emptying out rather than acquiring. It is an unveiling of what is always here. In the process, we lose everything we *think* we are. We usually begin this ground-level exploration with a constricted identity along with an inner grip of tension that we mis-take as our self. We enter standing upon the false ground of a separate self that at some point begins to give way.

Second, it is a journey of willingness rather than heroic will. Instead of slaying demons, we question our most cherished beliefs. Rather than arming ourself with magical weapons and potions, we disarm. Instead of finding our grip, we relax it. Instead of trying to direct and control, we learn to listen and follow. Rather than becoming a special somebody, we discover that we are no one and everything. This discovery allows us to simply be as we are.

Third, the journey of embodying spirit is open-ended; there's no finish line. Conditioning is endless. So, too, is the process of deconditioning our body-mind. There will always be some gap, however small, between our deepest knowing and how we think, feel, sense, and act. There will always be more unfolding, further refinement, and a greater capacity to embody our deepest knowing. As Shunryu Suzuki Roshi, the founder of San Francisco Zen Center, once said, "You are perfect as you are, *and* you could use a little improvement." We are always both whole and wounded, unconditioned and conditioned. There is always more to discover, even as the inner search for home comes to a close.

Finally, when we do more or less return from our underground journey, emptied and opened, humbled and simplified, we do not emerge with a holy grail or golden fleece. There are no diplomas or headlines in the local paper. Our ordinary life continues much as it always has. We do our job, tend to our family and friends, and care for

our community and planet in whatever way we can. We also spontaneously radiate an embodied presence that is of benefit to all beings.
Luminosity is also open-ended.

Thank you for engaging in this underground journey with me. I
wish you well as you more intimately discover your deepest ground!

Acknowledgments

This book was birthed from the ground of silence. And there have been many helpers along the way, seen and unseen. I am grateful to those who have played the roles of teachers, students, clients, and friends. You know who you are!

I am deeply grateful to my wife, Christiane, who has generously supported me during this lengthy birthing process.

And I am grateful to Tami Simon for her attuned trust, and for my Sounds True editors Lyric Dodson and Sarah Stanton, who helped refine this offering.

Explorations

Below is a list of exercises in this book for quick reference.

Notes

Chapter 4: Discovering Presence

1. Jalal al-Din Rumi, "The Guest House," in *The Essential Rumi*, trans. Coleman Barks (London: Penguin, 2004).
2. For a long list of peer-reviewed research projects associated with the Shamatha Project led by B. Alan Wallace and Clifford Saron, see centerforcontemplativeresearch.org/contemplative-science/the-shamatha-project/#, accessed February 21, 2024.
3. Ramana Maharshi, *Talks with Ramana Maharshi* (San Diego: Inner Directions, 2000); and Nisargadatta Maharaj, *I Am That*, 2nd American ed., revised (Durham, NC: Acorn Press, 2012).

Chapter 5: The Sense of Inner Knowing

1. Ed Yong, *An Immense World* (New York: Random House, 2022), 6.
2. Eugene Gendlin, *Focusing* (New York: Bantam, 1982).
3. John Welwood, *Towards a Psychology of Awakening: Buddhism, Psychotherapy and the Path of Personal and Spiritual Transformation* (Boston: Shambhala, 2002).
4. John Prendergast, *In Touch: How to Tune In to the Inner Guidance of Your Body and Trust Yourself* (Boulder, CO: Sounds True, 2015), 37–51.
5. Daniel Seigel, *Pocket Guide to Interpersonal Neurobiology: An Integrative Handbook of the Mind* (New York: W. W. Norton, 2012).

Chapter 6: Questioning Beliefs

1. Antonio Damasio, *Self Comes to Mind: Constructing the Conscious Brain* (New York: Vintage, 2012).
2. John Prendergast, *The Deep Heart: Our Portal to Presence* (Boulder, CO: Sounds True, 2019), 45–54.

Chapter 7: Seeing Through False Ground

1. John Prendergast, *In Touch: How to Tune In to the Inner Guidance of Your Body and Trust Yourself* (Boulder, CO: Sounds True, 2015), 114–15.
2. Peter Levine, *Waking the Tiger—Healing Trauma* (Berkeley, CA: North Atlantic Books, 1997).
3. Bessel van der Kolk, *The Body Keeps the Score: Brain, Mind, and Body in the Healing of Trauma* (New York: Viking, 2014).
4. Thomas Hübl, *Healing Collective Trauma: A Process for Healing Our Intergenerational and Cultural Wounds* (Boulder, CO: Sounds True, 2020).
5. Nisargadatta Maharaj, *I Am That* (Durham, NC: Acorn Press, 1973), vi.

Chapter 8: The Knot in the Belly

1. *Onoda: 10,000 Nights in the Jungle*, directed by Arthur Harari (Paris: Bathysphere, 2021). Despite many attempts to inform him, Lieutenant Onoda did not believe that the war was over until, three decades later, he received direct orders from his original commanding officer to surrender.
2. Richard Schwartz, *Internal Family Systems Therapy* (New York: Guilford Press, 2019) and *No Bad Parts: Healing Trauma and Restoring Wholeness with the Internal Family Systems Model* (Boulder, CO: Sounds True, 2021); Hal and Sidra Stone, *Embracing Ourselves: The Voice Dialogue Manual* (Novato, CA: New World Library, 1989).
3. Erika Hayasaki, "Identical Twins Hint at How Environments Change Gene Expression," *The Atlantic*, May 15, 2018.

4. Robert Sapolsky, *Behave: The Biology of Humans at Our Best and Worst* (New York: Penguin, 2018).

Chapter 9: Survival Fear I
1. A. H. Almaas (Hameed Ali), *Diamond Heart, Book 1: Elements of the Real in Man* (Boston: Shambhala, 2000).

Chapter 10: Survival Fear II
1. Thich Nhat Hanh, *Interbeing: The 14 Mindfulness Trainings of Engaged Buddhism*, 4th ed. (Berkeley, CA: Parallax Press, 2020).
2. John Prendergast, *The Deep Heart: Our Portal to Presence* (Boulder, CO: Sounds True, 2019), 51–52.

Chapter 11: Falling Open
1. John Prendergast, *The Deep Heart: Our Portal to Presence* (Boulder, CO: Sounds True, 2019), 26.
2. Reza Shah-Kazemi, *Paths to Transcendence: According to Shankara, Ibn Arabi, and Meister Eckhart* (Bloomington, IN: World Wisdom, 2006), 152.
3. John Prendergast, *In Touch: How to Tune In to the Inner Guidance of Your Body and Trust Yourself* (Boulder, CO: Sounds True, 2015), 123–37.

Chapter 12: Carl Jung's Underground Journey into the Collective Unconscious
1. Peter Kingsley, *Catafalque: Carl Jung and the End of Humanity* (London: Catafalque Press, 2018), 398.
2. See Bill Plotkin, *The Journey of Soul Initiation: A Field Guide for Visionaries, Evolutionaries, and Revolutionaries* (Novato, CA: New World Library, 2021), for a different mapping. While Plotkin admires Jung's pioneering work, he questions his use of alchemical symbols as an interpretive framework.
3. Carl Gustav Jung, *Memories, Dreams, Reflections* (New York: Vintage, 1989), 20.
4. Jung, 45.

5. Jung, 77.

6. Jung, 175.

7. Jung, 178.

8. Jung, 179.

9. Jung, 181.

10. Jung, 191.

11. Jung, 191.

12. Jung, 199.

13. Jung, 275.

14. Carl Gustav Jung, "The Holy Men of India," *Collected Works*, vol. 11, *Psychology and Religion: East and West*, pt. 8, ed. and trans. Gerhard Adler and R. F. C. Hull (Princeton, NJ: Princeton University Press, 1966), para. 952, 955.

15. Jung, "The Holy Men of India," para. 952.

16. Jung, para. 956.

17. Jung's concept of the Self as the totality of the conscious and unconscious correlates with the description of Saguṇa Brahman (the absolute with qualities) in the Upanishadic tradition. See Lionel Corbett, "Jung's Self and the Ātman of the Upaniṣads," in *Eastern Practices and Individuation: Essays by Jungian Analysts*, ed. Less Stein (New York: Chiron Press, 2022).

18. Thanks to Helge Osterhold, PhD, for fine-tuning this summary.

19. Carl Gustav Jung, *The Red Book: A Reader's Edition* (New York: W. W. Norton, 2012), 53, 61.

20. Jung, *The Red Book*, 61.

21. David Godman, *Be As You Are: The Teachings of Sri Ramana Maharshi* (London: Penguin UK, 1988), 1.

22. Lionel Corbett and Leanne Whitney, "Jung and Non-duality: Some Clinical and Theoretical Implications of the Self as Totality of the Psyche," *International Journal of Jungian Studies* 8, no. 1 (2016); John Prendergast, Peter Fenner, and Sheila Krystal, eds., *The Sacred Mirror: Nondual Wisdom and Psychotherapy* (St Paul, MN: Paragon House, 2003); and John Prendergast and Ken Bradford, eds., *Listening from the Heart of Silence, Vol. 2* (St. Paul, MN: Paragon House, 2007).

23. Carl Gustav Jung, *The Answer to Job* (Princeton, NJ: Princeton University Press, 2012), 108.

24. Kingsley, *Catafalque*, 418–19.

Chapter 13: Groundless Ground

1. "Chiyono's Enlightenment Poem," The Dewdrop, December 18, 2019, thedewdrop.org/2019/12/18/chiyonos-enlightenment-poem/.

2. Adyashanti, *The Direct Way: Thirty Practices to Evoke Awakening* (Boulder, CO: Sounds True, 2021), 54.

3. Adyashanti, *The Direct Way*, 55.

4. Adyashanti, 55.

Chapter 14: Landing HERE

1. Christopher Bache, *LSD and the Mind of the Universe: Diamonds from Heaven* (Rochester, VT: Park Street Press, 2019).

Chapter 15: The Upwelling Current of Life

1. Christopher Wallis, *The Recognition Sutras: Illuminating a 1,000-Year-Old Spiritual Masterpiece* (Boulder, CO: Mattamayūra Press, 2017).

2. Judith Blackstone, *The Fullness of the Ground: A Guide to Embodied Awakening* (Boulder, CO: Sounds True, 2023).

Chapter 16: Taking Your Seat

1. "Gate gate pāragate pārasamgate bodhi svāhā" is also translated as "Gone, gone, everyone gone to the other shore, awakening, svāhā." Wikipedia, s.v. "Heart Sutra," last modified June 20, 2024, en.wikipedia.org/wiki/Heart_Sutra.

2. Alert readers will notice the similarity of this saying with one of the lines in T. S. Eliot's "Little Gidding," where he directly quotes from the thirteenth-century Christian mystic Julian of Norwich: "All shall be well, and / All manner of thing shall be well." Yet Dame Julian was speaking of a future life in heaven rather than the present moment—a very important difference!

Additional Resources

Adyashanti. *The Direct Way: Thirty Practices to Evoke Awakening.* Boulder, CO: Sounds True, 2021.

———. *Emptiness Dancing.* Boulder, CO: Sounds True, 2006.

———. *The End of Your World: Uncensored Straight Talk on the Nature of Enlightenment.* Boulder, CO: Sounds True, 2010.

———. *The Way of Liberation: A Practical Guide to Spiritual Enlightenment.* San Jose, CA: Open Gate Sangha, 2013.

Almaas, A. H. *The Alchemy of Freedom: The Philosophers' Stone and the Secrets of Existence.* Boston: Shambhala, 2017.

———. *Facets of Unity.* Boston: Shambhala, 2002.

———. *Runaway Realization.* Boston: Shambhala, 2014.

———, and Karen Johnson. *The Power of Divine Eros: The Illuminating Force of Love in Everyday Life.* Boston: Shambhala, 2013.

Bache, Christopher M. *LSD and the Mind of the Universe: Diamonds from Heaven.* Rochester, VT: Park Street Press, 2019.

Blackstone, Judith. *The Fullness of the Ground: A Guide to Embodied Awakening.* Boulder, CO: Sounds True, 2023.

———. *Trauma and the Unbound Body: The Healing Power of Fundamental Consciousness.* Boulder, CO: Sounds True, 2019.

Bodian, Stephan. *Beyond Mindfulness: The Direct Approach to Lasting Peace, Happiness, and Love.* Oakland, CA: Nonduality Press, 2017.

Hanson, Rick. *Hardwiring Happiness: The New Brain Science of Contentment, Calm, and Confidence.* New York: Harmony, 2013.

————— with Forrest Hanson. *Resilient: How to Grow an Unshakable Core of Calm, Strength, and Happiness.* New York: Harmony, 2020.

Kelly, Loch. *Shift into Freedom: The Science and Practice of Open-Hearted Awareness.* Boulder, CO: Sounds True, 2015.

Kingsley, Peter. *Catafalque: Carl Jung and the End of Humanity.* London: Catafalque Press, 2018.

Klein, Jean. *Be Who You Are.* Salisbury, UK: Nonduality Press, 2006.

Levine, Peter A. *In an Unspoken Voice: How the Body Releases Trauma and Restores Goodness.* Berkeley, CA: North Atlantic Books, 2010.

————. *Waking the Tiger.* Berkeley, CA: North Atlantic Books, 1997.

Maharshi, Ramana. *Talks with Ramana Maharshi.* San Diego, CA: Inner Directions, 2000.

Morgan, Caverly. *The Heart of Who We Are: Realizing Freedom Together.* Boulder, CO: Sounds True, 2022.

Nhat Hahn, Thich. *Interbeing: The 14 Mindfulness Trainings of Engaged Buddhism.* 4th ed. Berkeley, CA: Parallax Press, 2020.

Plotkin, Bill. *The Journey of Soul Initiation: A Field Guide for Visionaries, Evolutionaries, and Revolutionaries.* Novato, CA: New World Library, 2021.

Prendergast, John. *The Deep Heart: Our Portal to Presence.* Boulder, CO: Sounds True, 2019.

————. *In Touch: How to Tune In to the Inner Guidance of Your Body and Trust Yourself.* Boulder, CO: Sounds True, 2015.

————, and G. Kenneth Bradford, eds. *Listening from the Heart of Silence: Nondual Wisdom and Psychotherapy, Vol. 2.* St. Paul, MN: Paragon House, 2007.

————, Peter G. Fenner, and Sheila Krystal, eds. *The Sacred Mirror: Nondual Wisdom and Psychotherapy.* St. Paul, MN: Paragon House, 2003.

Ray, Reginald A. *The Awakening Body: Somatic Meditation for Discovering Our Deepest Life.* Boston: Shambhala, 2016.

————. *Touching Enlightenment: Finding Realization in the Body.* Boulder, CO: Sounds True, 2014.

Sapolsky, Robert M. *Behave: The Biology of Humans at Our Best and Worst*. New York: Penguin, 2018.

Schwartz, Richard C. *Internal Family Systems*. New York: Guilford Press, 2019.

———. *No Bad Parts: Healing Trauma and Restoring Wholeness with the Internal Family Systems Model*. Boulder, CO: Sounds True, 2021.

Shah-Kazemi, Reza. *Paths to Transcendence: According to Shankara, Ibn Arabi, and Meister Eckhart*. Bloomington, IN: World Wisdom, 2006.

Siegel, Daniel J. *Aware: The Science and Practice of Presence*. New York: Tarcher Perigee, 2020.

———. *Pocket Guide to Interpersonal Neurobiology: An Integrative Handbook of the Mind*. New York: W. W. Norton, 2012.

Sapolsky, Robert M. *Behave: The Biology of Humans at Our Best and Worst*. New York: Penguin, 2018.

Spira, Rupert. *Being Aware of Being Aware*. Oxford: Sahaja Publications, 2017.

———. *Presence: The Art of Peace and Happiness*. Vol. 1. Oxford: Sahaja Publications, 2016.

———. *Transparent Body, Luminous World: The Tantric Yoga of Sensation and Perception*. Oxford: Sahaja Publications, 2015.

van der Kolk, Bessel. *How the Body Keeps the Score: Brain, Mind, and Body in the Healing of Trauma*. New York: Viking, 2014.

Wallis, Christopher. *The Recognition Sutras: Illuminating a 1,000-Year-Old Spiritual Masterpiece*. Petaluma, CA: Mattamayūra Press, 2017.

———. *Tantra Illuminated: The Philosopher, History, and Practice of a Timeless Tradition*. Petaluma, CA: Mattamayūra Press. 2013.

About the Author

John J. Prendergast, PhD, is the author of *The Deep Heart: Our Portal to Presence* and *In Touch: How to Tune In to the Inner Guidance of Your Body and Trust Yourself.* He is a retired adjunct professor of psychology at the California Institute of Integral Studies, where he taught and supervised master's level counseling students for twenty-three years. Now retired, he was also a licensed psychotherapist in private practice from 1986 to 2021.

John is the senior editor of and contributor to two anthologies of original essays: *The Sacred Mirror: Nondual Wisdom and Psychotherapy* (with Peter Fenner and Sheila Krystal) and *Listening from the Heart of Silence: Nondual Wisdom & Psychotherapy, Volume 2* (with Ken Bradford).

He studied for many years with the European sage Dr. Jean Klein and also Adyashanti, who offered him dharma transmission in 2023. John was also invited to share the dharma by Dorothy Hunt.

He lives in Petaluma, California, and offers in-person retreats in the United States and Europe with his wife, Christiane. He also offers online programs through various organizations. For more, please visit listeningfromsilence.com.

About Sounds True

Sounds True was founded in 1985 by Tami Simon with a clear mission: to disseminate spiritual wisdom. Since starting out as a project with one woman and her tape recorder, we have grown into a multimedia publishing company with a catalog of more than 3,000 titles by some of the leading teachers and visionaries of our time, and an ever-expanding family of beloved customers from across the world.

In more than three decades of evolution, Sounds True has maintained our focus on our overriding purpose and mission: to wake up the world. We offer books, audio programs, online learning experiences, and in-person events to support your personal growth and awakening, and to unlock our greatest human capacities to love and serve.

At SoundsTrue.com you'll find a wealth of resources to enrich your journey, including our weekly *Insights at the Edge* podcast, free downloads, and information about our nonprofit Sounds True Foundation, where we strive to remove financial barriers to the materials we publish through scholarships and donations worldwide.

To learn more, please visit SoundsTrue.com/freegifts or call us toll-free at 800.333.9185.

Together, we can wake up the world.